Black

Introduction to the Phonology of English for Teachers of ESOL

by

Ray Parker
&
Tim Graham

ELB Publishing
31 George Street
Brighton
East Sussex
BN2 1RH

No unauthorised photocopying

First Published 1994

This edition 2002

0 95228082 5

© Ray Parker & Tim Graham 2002

CONTENTS

Acknowledgements

The authors would like to acknowledge the very valuable assistance of Alice Oxholm in the completion of this book. Her constant gentle encouragement, helpful comments and setting of deadlines were much appreciated. We should also like to extend our gratitude to Marion Graham for her careful proof-reading and Cathy Marples for her work in retyping the paper and electronic version of this revised edition.

Ray Parker
Tim Graham

Sheffield & London
2002

Introduction

This book was written with a specific readership in mind – native and non-native speakers of English who are planning or training to be Teachers of English to Speakers of Other Languages. If others find a use for it we are delighted but it is to this group that most of the issues raised will be important.

The book tries to cover all important aspects of the pronunciation of English and goes on to help people to prepare for qualifying examinations in this area which often require a basic knowledge of articulatory phonetics and the ability to transcribe accurately into and out of phonemic script.

The organisation of the book is the opposite to most similar works. We have adopted a "top-down" approach, starting with the broadest issues, then looking at suprasegmentals – intonation, stress etc, before taking a more atomistic view of phonemes and the articulatory mechanisms associated with them. It seems to us that the broader issues help to justify an interest in the narrower ones and thus, logically, should be covered first.

Each of the first twelve chapters has a 'Classroom Applications' section which we include, not only to enrich new teachers' repertoires of classroom techniques but as a constant reminder that pronunciation work is essentially practical.

We feel strongly that teachers need (from a personal point of view) a sound grasp of the theoretical framework of a system like the phonology of a language but that, without some practical means of passing on essential information to learners, such theoretical knowledge may contribute to the distancing of teachers from learners, instead of reducing it.

Chapters are preceded by a list of points to be covered and followed by a summary – either page can be used to assess the value of a particular chapter to the reader. You may well find a route through the chapters other than the sequence that we appear to be prescribing. This is your book now, not ours! To allow for this we have tended to write each part of the book so that it can 'stand alone'. This leads to some repetition, but at least offers a reasonably safe passage to those not passing through in chapter order.

In this new edition of the book we have added two postscripts. One on the notion of 'leaner accent' and what we should be aiming for as regards communicative intelligibility in a world where increasingly interactions in English are between non-native speakers and the implications that this has for the teacher of ESOL. This is dealt with briefly in Chapter One and developed further in the new postscript.

There is another short new chapter that aims to give the reader some insight into the type of question they may encounter when undertaking the oral interview section of the Trinity College London LTCL Diploma in TESOL. That part of the examination focuses specifically on phonology and in our second new postscript a few illustrative answers are given.

Finally we have added a glossary to reinforce definitions of terminology (we have tried not to use technical language undefined within the text but if you are not using the book in its original sequence you may well come across such words before they have been explained) and a bibliography for those who wish to explore further in this rich and rewarding area.

Note: Throughout the book when you see this symbol you can click to hear a spoken version of examples and exercises. There is also a useful list of the phonemic symbols with spoken examples. You may find this helpful in completing some of the tasks and exercises.

Claims that are not made for this book

1. This book is not a textbook on phonetics. There are plenty of these already published and examples of those that we have found particularly useful are included in the bibliography.

2. No claim can be made for this book in terms of absolute accuracy or completeness of description. Obviously we have taken every care to be as accurate as possible but the book contains many matters which are susceptible to much more detailed analysis than can be justified in a book of this type.

3. The book is not intended to be authoritative in the traditional sense. There are features in it that we know will be helpful to teachers approaching these matters for the first time but we fully expect readers to interact with the text to find their own attitudes, degrees of concern etc rather than simply swallowing ours.

The authors apologise in advance for those parts of the book where they seem to be speaking 'ex cathedra' and can only plead as an excuse their concern for economy and clarity.

Typological conventions

Please note the following typological conventions used throughout the book.

/ /   slashes are used to enclose material of phonemic significance

[ ]   square brackets are used to enclose material of phonetic significance

' '   inverted commas are used to enclose orthographic material e.g. letters of the alphabet

*   an asterisk placed in front of an utterance indicates that it is an unacceptable utterance for a native speaker

he/she   these pronouns have been used randomly throughout the book to refer to teachers and learners

bold   most terms in bold can be found as definitions in the glossary

Chapter One

Phonological objectives in a communicative language teaching programme

What this chapter includes

1.1 the need for teachers to take an informed interest in their learners' pronunciation

1.2 the competing claims of fluency and accuracy within the general context of pronunciation teaching and acquisition

1.3 degrees of intelligibility

1.4 the question of accent (or, rather, two questions!)

1.5 the setting of priorities when selecting phonological teaching/learning objectives

1.6 applications

1.7 summary

1.1 Why was this book written?

The answer to this question is easy. The vast majority of English Language teaching materials are in printed form. Indeed, supplying the world's learners of English with the materials they need is an undertaking that nearly all major educational publishers take very seriously indeed. Fortunately most major textbooks have accompanying tapes but, nevertheless, it is first and foremost the teacher who provides learners with their most accessible model of pronunciation and it is the teacher who is most likely to be offering advice, help, encouragement and criticism as the learner gradually gains more and more expertise in the pronunciation of the language.

So, not only are teachers very much in the frontline of pronunciation teaching but in many ways we are poorly supported in this area in terms of the ready-made materials on our shelves. Most coursebooks, naturally, only address themselves to a part of the language – e.g. 3rd year, upper intermediate, or preparation for a popular public examination like the UCLES First Certificate in English. Those, therefore, that attempt to integrate pronunciation into their partial syllabuses inevitably only provide practice in a part of the pronunciation of the language.

Unfortunately, our learners do not usually seem to acquire pronunciation skills in the same sequence or at the same time that coursebook writers extend their helping hand. It follows, then, that teachers must constantly be prepared to supplement and/or replace both the pronunciation topic of a particular unit in a coursebook and the manner in which it is tackled.

To achieve this confidently it is obviously wise to know:

(a)   what the pronunciation of English is really like

(b)   how it can be broken down into small enough chunks for learners to get a sense of achievement and progress

(c)   what degree of achievement we are aiming at.

This book is about (a) and (b) and the rest of this chapter will deal with (c).

1.2 Accuracy and fluency

For many years now teachers have been debating, amongst other important issues, the relative importance of accuracy and fluency as characteristics of their learners' eventual mastery of the target languages concerned. Though debate is a healthy sign in any profession, one unfortunate side-effect is a tendency amongst the debaters towards polarisation. Thus, in moments of passion the 'accuracy school' may suggest that the production of fluent but inaccurate speakers of languages is at best sloppy and at worst a form of charlatanism. The 'fluency school', equally passionately, may counter that inaccuracy is an essential stage in the language acquisition process and that the available evidence from studies of infants acquiring their native languages suggests that inaccuracy is transitory. They back up their claims with classroom observations that tend to confirm the idea that an excessive concern with accuracy may actually inhibit the development of fluency.

When we consider the phonology of a language, however, it seems to be impossible to maintain an entrenched position on either side.

From the point of view of expecting the pronunciation of a speaker to contribute to his communicative effectiveness, someone who speaks fluently but with lots of wrong sounds in the speech stream is going to be as unintelligible as someone who speaks in a disjointed and hesitant way but with the right sounds is going to be tiresome and taxing to listen to. Neither is going to be communicatively successful. What's more if, as many linguists believe, the language model they present when speaking is a reflection of the listening strategies they employ, then they are both also going to have great difficulty understanding authentic samples of the language.

For our purposes a reasonable balance between these two features of proficiency would seem to be desirable – but with one proviso. That is that to some extent accuracy and fluency in speech cannot always be seen as separate or separable (still less as mutually exclusive) features. There is a strong case to be made for the notion that accuracy can be a component of fluency. One cannot be fluent in a language simply by being unhesitating, ready, quick – one must also be intelligible if any communicative purpose is to be achieved and this requires a reasonable degree of accuracy, which, naturally enough, leads to the question.......

1.3.1   What constitutes a reasonable degree of accuracy?

Ultimately, the answer to this in a communicative sense is that degree of accuracy which enables the speaker to effectively get their message across. Accuracy then, is not an absolute concept. The point at which a student has attained sufficient accuracy is going to be a matter of professional judgement on the teacher's part. As you progress through the chapters of this book you will come across any number of features of the pronunciation of English which could cause problems for our learners. At every step you will need to ask yourself – both in your reading of this book and in the classroom – how far should I go in deliberately insisting on this matter? If my students don't quite master this sound or that feature of connected speech, will they fail to make themselves understood?

We can probably distinguish various stages in the acquisition of a particular sound or feature of connected speech and for argument's sake we have set out four stages below.

1.   gross inaccuracy

2.   approximate accuracy

3.   near mastery

4.   mastery

However, learners do not, of course, acquire the whole phonology of a foreign language evenly or, indeed, identically. Particular learners will demonstrate particular difficulties with particular sounds or features of pronunciation. This will depend on their own native language, the age at which they started learning English, the model(s) to which they have been previously exposed, their own and their society's attitude towards English etc, etc.

You may well find as a result of all this that you will have to settle for different levels of attainment for different parts of the pronunciation of the language. This may be particularly true as the law of diminishing returns begins to apply and you find that to squeeze out the last drop of accuracy in a student's performance involves you and him in such a burden of practice and remedial work that he gets demoralised, or worse still, too embarrassed to speak freely.

1.3.2 Intelligibility

We have so far allowed ourselves to use this word without defining it. It is important, however, to look at it carefully as it may not mean in our context precisely what it does to the layperson. The concept of intelligibility is straightforward enough in itself but the issue which must preoccupy us a little is – intelligibility to whom? In other words, when we say that we want our students to be intelligible, do we mean intelligible to us, or to other less linguistically aware native speakers of English, or – as English becomes more and more a means of international communication – to other non-native users of English (See Postscript 1). There is a world of difference here.

This difference can be described as tolerance. We don't mean here, of course, tolerance in the sense of an accepting, uncritical attitude, but tolerance in a more linguistic sense. The ability to decode poorly realised pronunciation, to unconsciously or consciously reformulate while listening to inaccurate sounds or deviant features. This is an ability that experienced teachers of ESOL develop to a high degree. It is a skill that all native speakers share to some extent. It is skill, however, that tends to be minimally developed in those who are approaching the language as learners.

Thus we can range different groups of people according to the degree of tolerance at their disposal.

(1)   **Degree of tolerance**   **Type of listener**
            Very tolerant

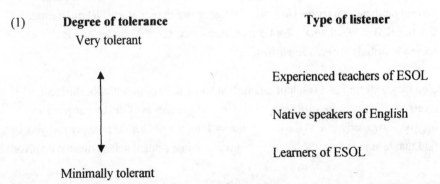

Experienced teachers of ESOL

Native speakers of English

Learners of ESOL

            Minimally tolerant

Now, if we compare that scale of listeners with our earlier scale of degrees of mastery an important implication should become clear.

(2)   **Type of listener:**   **Degree of proficiency**
       needed   **for communication to take**
                                               place in a reasonably effective
                                               and relaxed way:

                                               Gross inaccuracy

Experienced teachers of ESOL

                                               Approximate accuracy

Native speakers of English

                                               Near mastery

Other learners of ESOL

                                               Mastery

In case you haven't spotted it, the implication is that we should not rely too much on seeking a level of achievement in pronunciation that equates with intelligibility to us. We are too tolerant, too skilled at negotiating meaning with our learners, too good at interpreting their inaccuracies because we want to encourage them. We need frequently to remind ourselves that to be intelligible to us may well not be enough for our learners. We may often have to aim at levels of accuracy and fluency well beyond what **we** need in order to understand our learners if they are to be effective communicators outside the sheltered environment of the classroom.

1.4.1   What accent should a teacher of English have?

The answer to this question really is easy – his or her own. It is important, however, to state this since books like this one are often guilty of giving an impression not intended by their writers. The problem is that there is no scope in a book of this size to deal with the astounding richness of regional variation of accent that English, like many other languages, has to offer. As an inevitable result of this all the material in the following chapters refers to a single accent. It happens to be approximately that of the authors and is generally referred to as Received Pronunciation or R.P. for short.

The authors make no claim whatever about the merit of this particular accent over any other. Unlike most accents, however, it does not have a clearly defined regional base. Thus whereas a South Yorkshire accent or a Johannesburg accent may tell you something about the geographical origins of its owner, an R.P. accent doesn't. This is not an advantage or a disadvantage – just a fact. Nobody should attempt to "put on" a particular accent in the classroom. It is hard enough routinely presenting students with undistorted models of the language without adding the burden of doing so in someone else's accent.

These remarks will upset a dwindling minority of traditionalists who associate the "Queen's English" – by which they tend to mean R.P. – with other aspects of the language of which we might justifiably feel a little proud. But from a strictly scientific point of view no particular accent can ever be claimed to be intrinsically better or worse than any other. Similarly no accent should be described as being "stronger" or "purer" or "more neutral" than any other. These are simply not adjectives you can apply to accents.

At the beginning of this chapter it was suggested that there were two questions here, not one – so let's look at the other side of the coin:-

1.4.2   What accent should our students have?

This question is not quite so simple as the one before. Indeed our students may have a more legitimate right to answer this one than we have. For reasons beyond our proper control they may be hell-bent on acquiring R.P. or as near to a native British accent as possible, or they may perceive a North American accent as their ideal. Alternatively, of course, they may not have a goal in these terms at all. In a sense, our position should be as neutral as possible, but it is worth bearing in mind that, as English continues to become more and more the international language, it arguably becomes less and less the exclusive property of those who happen to acquire it the easy way – from birth. In other words we are rapidly approaching an era when non-native accents of English are beginning to achieve a status comparable to native accents. We may not be far away from the time when, in an international setting, a French accent is as acceptable (and perhaps as intelligible) as a Birmingham accent, a Japanese accent could rival an Australian accent in terms of prestige, etc, etc.

In short, it is reasonable to expect that for most of our learners, their use of English will not be part of an overall plan to pass themselves off as English (or American etc) people, but rather part of an attempt to express themselves in English. If this means retaining an overlay of foreign accent – so long as this does not adversely affect their communicative purposes – so be it.

1.5 Communicative priorities in the teaching of pronunciation

As has been implied in the sections on accuracy and fluency not all pronunciation targets and not all pronunciation problems can be seen as having equal status in a language teaching programme. This is particularly true when the syllabus or the teacher is taking a communicative view of the learner's purpose and progress.

As a very general rule of thumb, it can be claimed in English that the broader the level of phonology analysis, the more serious the communicative consequences of non-acquisition. Thus 'big' features of pronunciation like intonation, rhythm and stress would seem to have greater communicative value than smaller single sound features.

It is well known that Japanese learners of English (among others) tend to have great difficulty in some contexts distinguishing between the sounds that we represent in writing with the letters 'r' and 'i'. Hence the music-hall type jokes about 'flied lice' etc. Less well known (probably because it provides less easily exploitable material to comedians) is the difficulty they have with rhythm when speaking whole sentences in English.

Experienced teachers often find that a relatively small amount of work on the latter feature brings with it all sorts of hidden benefits, especially in terms of unstressed vowel qualities, (see Chapter 4) whereas the former problem requires lengthy, repeated and very skilful handling. Even when this is successful (by no means always the case) there is little actual improvement in communicative efficiency, which in any case was probably not really threatened in the first place (see Chapter 6).

1.6   Applications

1.6.1   Group unjumbling

The class is a mixed nationality EFL group of young adults in the UK. There are 16 of them and they are at an intermediate level.

The teacher has written a simple 8 line dialogue as follows:

Have you seen that cassette my mother left here last week?

It was on top of the hi-fi.

Well it's not there now.

Well I haven't moved it – perhaps Susan …..

You're right – I'll go and look in her room.

No, tell **her** to look – she knows where she puts things.

I can't. She's next door playing with their children.

Well, call her – it's time for lunch anyway.

She has written the dialogue twice and then cut it up into one line strips which she has shuffled. She divides the class into two groups of eight and gets each group to rearrange their chairs into a semicircle. She then distributes one line of the dialogue to each member of the class taking care to ensure that each group has a complete dialogue between them. She instructs them not to show their strips to each other but, to memorise their one line. After a minute she collects up the strips of paper and tells the groups that without any further intervention from her they should now tell each other what their lines are and rearrange themselves in their semicircles until they are satisfied that they have reconstructed a coherently sequenced conversation.

There is an animated discussion for 15 minutes. Students listen intensely to each other and frequently correct each other's pronunciation or request several repetitions until they have successfully decoded a class-mate's accent. After 15 minutes, then, the two groups seem to have decided on a sequence. The teacher then announces that there is to be a dictation. Again, however, she says that she'll be taking a back seat. They'll do the dictation in groups with each person dictating their own line. By the end of the dictation they should each have the whole dialogue written down. Unlike more formal dictations, they are told that they can request as many repetitions as they want, but, of course, they mustn't look at each other's writing. There follows a further 10 minutes of very intensive and active 'dictation'.

At the end of this period the teacher distributes a handout with the original dialogue on it and as the class members compare their versions with the original she monitors them and joins in discussions about how any changes they have generated during the whole process have altered, spoilt or actually improved the original.

What is gained by using techniques like this?

The most important gain is the raising of the level of awareness amongst the learners of their own communicative effectiveness. The successful completion of a task like this depends on each member of the group being intelligible to each of the others. Additionally, the teacher gains useful information about the relative intelligibility of her students. Finally, because of the in-built need to successfully complete the task there is a real incentive for members of the group, finding themselves misunderstood or not understood at all, to actually modify their pronunciation in the direction of intelligibility. Learners can lack a sense of what communicative intelligibility truly is and consequently demote pronunciation for the sake of, say, grammatical accuracy. This is a misapprehension. Without a reasonable degree of phonological accuracy, grammatical exactitude is likely to be seriously compromised.

1.6.2   Reading aloud in the class

There are very mixed feelings in the TESOL profession about the merits and disadvantages of activities of this kind.

Those who are against it argue that:

(a)   it is potentially very stressful for the readers.

(b)   it is a rather special skill that native speakers seldom actually employ in their own languages and which is even less frequently needed in a foreign language.

(c)   as part of a general teaching strategy it is apparently ineffective (this is something which seems often to be true of techniques which can be seen to test rather than teach).

Those who are for it claim that:

(a)   it figures in many state language syllabuses as a skill that their learners are required in some degree to master.

(b)   their learners actually enjoy doing it.

(c)   it makes reading lessons more active and participative.

However you view these arguments we ought to add that in the context of this chapter and book (i.e. the teaching of pronunciation skills in a **communicative** context) there is no logical defence for this technique. It is also worth noting that such a technique probably has more of a detrimental effect than a positive one given the nature of the English spelling system (see Chapter 7(7.1))

1.7 Summary

This chapter has set out to examine a number of issues that can be seen as the partial application in a communicative setting of matters to be dealt with in more detail in the chapters that follow.

Specifically we have looked at:

- the reasons for teachers being informed about the phonology of the language they are teaching

- the concepts of accuracy and fluency applied to phonological performance

- intelligibility

- communicative priorities

- the question of accent for teachers and learners (see also Postscript 1)

In the applications section we have looked at:

- group unjumbling

- reading aloud in the class

Chapter Two

Suprasegmental phonology: an overview

What this chapter includes

2.1 A brief introduction

As stated already, in this book we adopt a 'top-down' approach to the analysis of phonology. In other words, we start with the 'whole' and work to the 'parts'. In this chapter, then, we shall be considering some of the major aspects of English phonology, particularly **intonation**. The four subsequent chapters will deal with aspects of suprasegmental phonology in some depth. This chapter will act as an introduction to these aspects.

2.2 Suprasegmental phonology

Suprasegmental phonology, as the name suggests, is concerned with features above the level of the segment. So, for the moment, we will not worry about the particular nature of the   't-sound' in 'eighth' for example, or how the '-ed' in 'pointed' is pronounced – these are only segments of the words. We shall be considering such segmental phenomena later. In the next few chapters our concern will be only with words, phrases and sentences and the sound patterns that are associated with them. In order to do this however, there is, ironically, one 'part' we must consider: the syllable.

2.3 The syllable

Most speakers will have an intuitive understanding of what a syllable is, even though they may not have consciously thought about it. If we take, for example, the words 'butt' and 'butter' no-one would disagree that one of the things that makes them different (and hence allows them to carry different meanings) is the fact that 'butt' has only one syllable (i.e. it is **monosyllabic**) whilst 'butter' has two (it is **disyllabic**). So far so good. However, even though we can trust our instincts on this point and be reasonably confident of being able to count the number of syllables in a given word, actually arriving at a satisfactory definition of what a syllable is, is not so simple a matter. It is not our purpose here to enter into the debate of what does and what does not constitute a syllable. Rather we shall confine ourselves to a general working definition.

If we take again as an example the word 'butt', which we said has only one syllable, we can begin to get an idea of the principles involved.

In the word 'butt' there is a 'b-sound', a 't-sound' and a vowel sound. A vowel sound is a sound where there is a relatively free air-flow from the lungs and out through the mouth. If you contrast the way that the air escapes for the three sounds in 'butt', you will discover that for the 'b-' and 't-sounds' the airflow is not free and that the actual production of these sounds relies, in part, on some form of direct obstruction. A syllable, in the vast majority of cases, must have a vowel sound. Furthermore, the vowel sound must form the centre or nucleus of the syllable. On the other hand, a syllable need not contain consonant sounds (a consonant sound is an obstructed air-flow sound like the b and the t in 'butt'). The word 'eye', which is monosyllabic, consists of a vowel sound alone. We could call such syllables **basic** or, as Roach (1983) does, **minimum**. They have neither an **onset** (an initial consonant sound) or **termination** (i.e. a final consonant sound). In other words they are not bordered by consonant sounds. Of course, it follows that we can have syllables that do have onset but no termination (e.g. 'two') or syllables that have a termination but no onset (e.g. 'it'). What syllables do have in common is a vowel sound and the pulse from the lungs that produces them. This pulsing can be heard if you place your fingers in your ears and say some short words or phrases.

Try counting the number of syllables in the following words:

Ex. 1

Examples:	meet (1)	wonder (2)	aeroplane (3)
	one ( )	seven ( )	inspection ( )
	introspection ( )	television ( )	cat ( )
	nomad ( )	commercialisation ( )	psychiatry ( )

2.4 Stress and the syllable

Now we have looked at the syllable we can begin to appreciate how words, phrases and sentences are patterned. We saw that one of the phonological differences between 'butt' and 'butter' is the fact that the former has one syllable and the latter two. We can now consider another feature of suprasegmental phonology: **stress**. In the word 'butter' we can perceive not only that there are two syllables, but also that these two syllables differ from each other in terms of **prominence**. It should be clear that the more prominent syllable of the two is the first – the 'bu-' rather than the '-tter'. (The reason for the division of the syllables in this way will be dealt with later (see Chapter 3 (3.5)).) If you try making the second syllable more prominent, you will find that the word loses its phonological shape and consequently sounds 'odd'. However, some nouns and verbs in English are distinguished by this same process. Consider the noun 'import' where the first syllable is the prominent one, and the verb 'import' where the second is the stronger. This is, though, relatively rare and most words have a fixed sound pattern. This is known as **word stress** and will be discussed in Chapter 3. Word stress often causes problems for learners, particularly in the case of proper nouns. We have probably all come across an English place or street name with which we are unfamiliar and wondered where to put the stress – Arundel, for example. This is a problem that learners face all the time and can prove to be very frustrating. Coming to terms with word stress and developing a sensitivity to learners' difficulties in this area are important skills for the ESOL teacher to develop.

 Ex. 2

Identify the stressed syllable in these words and underline it:

Examples: a<u>dorn</u>   <u>je</u>ster   <u>cu</u>shion

            even   rugged   protest (!)   people

            support   parent   appeal   kidnap

Since words themselves carry a stress, it follows that phrases and sentences must too. English is often characterised as a **stress-timed** language. In effect, this means that the rhythm of English sentences is determined by a regular 'beat', rather like a drum-beat accompanying a piece of music. This phenomenon will be dealt with in Chapter 4, but we can consider some preliminary examples.

When we are conveying a message, we naturally, though usually subconsciously, draw attention to the important items in that message. Again, though we are probably not aware of it, these items stand out from others in the message. This brings us to the concept of **content words** and **function words**. Content words are essential to meaning and when we speak, they receive greater prominence or stress. They tend to be nouns, verbs, adverbs and adjectives. Function words, although still significant to the overall message, are given rather less attention and value and as a rule do not stand out. These tend to be prepositions, articles, pronouns, conjunctions and certain auxiliary verbs.

Say the sentence:

Mr Smith was surprised to find that all the pies had gone.

With practice you should be able to detect the regular beat, which is, as we said above, an important feature of spoken English. You should also be able to hear that this beat has the effect of weakening certain words – in fact, the function words.

Say the word: 'was' in isolation and then say the sentence above again. You should find that the 'was' in the sentence has a rather different quality than the 'was' in isolation. This is something we shall return to later (see Chapter 4 (4.1)). It is sufficient for now that you are aware that there is something 'going on' when words combine to form sentences.

In case you are not sure, the syllables that carry the beat in the sentence discussed are capitalised below:

MISter SMITH was surPRISED to FIND that ALL the PIES had GONE.

One technique that might help you in identifying the beats in the sentence is to tap out a steady rhythm as you say it.

Like word-stress, sentence-stress may be problematic for learners. Many languages are not stress-timed. French, for example, is syllable-timed, which, to English speaking ears (!) gives it a staccato effect. This is because the function words are not 'weakened' in the same way as they are in English. To give you an idea of this, consider an onomatopoeic English phrase which by its nature approaches syllable-timing. It is taken from Wilfred Owen's poem 'Anthem for the Doomed Youth'.

'Only the stuttering rifles' rapid rattle ...'

Owen attempts here to mimic the sound of rifle fire. The type of sound pattern he creates is typical of syllable-timed languages and is a series of alternating stressed and unstressed syllables. It is, however, atypical of English, which is what gives it its poetic effect. A somewhat lighter example is the last line of the Carolyn West limerick which concludes:

But I'd hate to relate,
What that fellow named Tate
And his tete-a-tete ate at 8.08 (eight eight).

If we, as English speakers, find such staccato speech patterns unusual then we must be aware that learners from non-stress-timed languages will have the same problem in reverse. Some techniques for dealing with this are mentioned in the section on applications.

Since English is a stress-timed language, English speakers have the facility to encode messages by placing stress in a particular way. An example of this might be:

A: What's his name?
B: What's her name, you mean. She's a woman.

where the 'her' in 'What's her name?' would be the prominent item. By contrast, the prominent item in 'What's his name?' would normally be 'name', with 'his' being weak. This is known as **contrastive stress** and will be considered in Chapter 6. Many languages do not share this facility and in order to draw attention to a particular item have to resort to periphrasis (see Chapter 6, section 6.3 for examples of this phenomenon taken from Spanish) or changes in word order.

2.5 Intonation

We are now ready to consider one of the fundamentals of English phonology – **intonation**. Intonation is the overall pattern of sound that is associated with a given message or part of that message. Intonation is related to stress but has a direct bearing on meaning too. We have probably all heard the expression: "Don't speak to me in that tone of voice". What the speaker is usually objecting to is the intonation pattern used by the 'offender'. It is perhaps apt here to draw a parallel with music. The intonation of English may be viewed as a type of modulation or tune. If you say the sentence we looked at above:

Mr Smith was surprised to find that all the pies had gone.

the musical analogy might not be immediately clear. However, if you do not articulate it, but simply hum it, the correlation is clearer. There is a kind of lilting melody that gently rises on the syllable '-prised' and then gradually falls in pitch. The most noticeable fall is on the word 'gone'. This tune, or rise and fall of pitch, is what we refer to as intonation and will be discussed in Chapter 5.

Intonation is one aspect of the language where the teacher tends to have to cope alone. Most coursebooks skirt around the issue and as a phenomenon it is difficult to satisfactorily demonstrate except via direct teacher-led practice.

Try saying the words: "Give me a pen" first as an emphatic order and then as an informal polite request. Now convert these to tunes. You will find that the tunes are quite different. This subtle yet crucial feature of the language is something that all native English speakers can do naturally; yet when it comes to teaching, it requires careful thought. Normal writing conventions are not an accurate guide to intonation patterns, though in some cases they may approximate to them. Intonation can and does operate at word, phrase and whole sentence level. One particular sentence might have a single unbroken tune; on the other hand, it might have more than one.

Compare:

"What's his name?"

where we have one unbroken tune (or more properly one **intonation group**) with a fall on 'name', and:

"What's his name and what does he want?"

We can detect, with a bit of practice perhaps, that in the second example we have one sentence but two tunes – two intonation groups. The second sentence has an initial intonation group similar to that of the first sentence, but this time with a slight rise on 'name' rather than a fall. It then has a subsequent group beginning 'and...' with a fall on 'want'. We could in fact break up the second sentence thus:

‖ What's his name | and what does he want? ‖

where the double vertical lines represent the complete utterance/sentence and the single vertical line represents the boundary between intonation groups. A similar division could be made for the 'Mr Smith' – sentence above, the division following the word 'find'. What then determines what an intonation group is?

2.6   Intonation groups

As we discussed above, an intonation group, by analogy with music, consists of a single unbroken tune. In English such a group is conventionally deconstructed into four specific sections. These are the **nucleus**, the **head**, the **pre-head** and the **tail**. This probably sounds a little jargonistic but it is a relatively simple concept to grasp.

The single most prominent syllable in an intonation group – the one that, in effect, determines a falling or rising tune – is called the **nucleus**. The nucleus is usually thought of, and perceived as, the most important item in a given message (again normally at a subconscious level).

The change of pitch that the nucleus initiates and which stretches to the end of the intonation group is referred to as the **nuclear tone**.

In the sentence spoken by B in the exchange:

A: "When did you say you arrived?"

B: "I arrived on Friday."

the nucleus will be on the syllable 'Fri-', because 'Fri-', distinguishes the day from 'Mon-', 'Wednes-', 'Thurs-' etc, and is also the most significant item of B's response. To demonstrate this point say the B sentence again, this time with 'I' as the most prominent item. The result is not a direct reply to A's question. It suggests that B is answering the question:

"Who arrived on Friday?"

The 'neutral response' – i.e. the one that gives the information requested and nothing more – is with 'Fri-' as the nucleus.

In this book we will need only to deal with the nucleus of an intonation group and its tune and the head. The head of an intonation group stretches from the first stressed syllable in the group to the nucleus. Just out of interest, the pre-head consists of any unstressed syllables that precede the head, and the tail consists of those syllables (if there are any) that follow the nucleus. Take the example:

A packet of biscuits.

where 'a' is the pre-head, 'packet of' is the head, 'bis' is the nucleus and '-cuits' is the tail.

 Ex. 3

Underline the nucleus in the following sentences, as spoken in a neutral way:

Examples: My name's <u>Fred</u>   I'm a <u>tour</u>ist.

What do you <u>mean</u>?

What's your name?   Is it time to go?

How do you do?   Can I come in?

Would you like some tea?   What would you like to drink?

24

When you have identified the nuclei of these sentences, think about the tune they have. Do they go up (rise) or do they go down (fall) in terms of pitch? You should find that, even though they are all questions, certain nuclei rise and others naturally fall. As a rule of thumb (and admittedly this is something of a simplification) we can say that **Wh- questions** (who, what, where, when, how, why etc) have a falling tone/tune, whilst **polar questions** (those requiring a yes/no answer) have a rising tone.

Statements of fact tend to have a falling nuclear tone, whereas unfinished lists, requests for clarification (You went where?) and items of **phatic communion** (in essence, things that keep a conversation going – "mmmmm?", "Really?" etc) have a rising nuclear tone.

Consider the list:

|| one | two | three | four | five ||

where each item has its own intonation group and hence its own tune. You should be able to detect rises on each of the first four items, followed by a fall on 'five'. The fall indicates that the list is complete.

The same is true of the second example below:

1.   "What would you like to drink? Vodka, Scotch, rum .....?"
       (note the orthographic convention here ".....".)

2.   "What would you like to drink? Vodka or gin?"

In example 1 the speaker conveys the fact that there are other choices available as well as those mentioned. Compare the tone 1 with that for 2 where the last item of the list, 'gin', has a falling tone. This signals that gin is the only other choice to vodka. In the first example the list is, in fact, unfinished. In the second example it is complete.

Intonation patterns and their significance will be dealt with more fully in Chapter 6.

2.7 Presenting this information to learners

Intonation, as we have discussed, is an important aspect of spoken English. English teachers, therefore, need a fair working knowledge of how intonation operates not only at word-stress level, but also at sentence level. How then would the teacher demonstrate such linguistic features?

One technique is to use the orthographic script to try to emulate stress and intonation. There are various ways of doing this:

At word-stress level:

Using a short vertical line ' to indicate the stressed syllable:

e.g.   com'bine   into'nation   'quarrel

Note that the line precedes the syllable that carries the stress.

Using a box to indicate the stressed syllable:

□   □   □

e.g.   combine   intonation   quarrel

Using capital letters to indicate the stressed syllable:

e.g.   comBINE   intoNAtion   QUArrel

Underling the stressed syllable:

e.g.   com<u>bine</u>   into<u>na</u>tion   <u>qua</u>rrel

Similar conventions apply to marking sentence stress. In this book we will be using two systems for marking stress and intonation which, whilst not perfect, are relatively flexible and are used by many teachers in the classroom. These are boxes to indicate the syllables that carry stress in a given sentence:

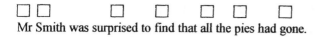
Mr Smith was surprised to find that all the pies had gone.

This system is useful when we are concerned only with stress and the overall rhythm of a sentence.

The other system employs circles to indicate unstressed syllables, stressed syllables and the nucleus. The circle representing the nucleus conventionally has a line attached to it to indicate the direction of the nuclear tone, thus:

●● ● ● ● ● ● ● ● ● ● ● ●
Mr   Smith was surprised to find that all the pies had gone.

This is fine as regards visual representation of stress, but another method is simply to exploit the teacher's own voice or to use recorded material and drill stress and intonation patterns through repetition and imitation. There is a good deal of pre-recorded material available for use with learners of English, but in order to exploit it effectively for phonological purposes it requires careful selection. Much of the material around is not overly authentic and often the teacher's demonstration will be more apposite. Using taped material (particularly in the form of video, as it provides broader context and more visual clues – lip movements/facial expression/gesture etc) does have the advantage of providing a fixed model for repetition-type exercises (notoriously difficult for the teacher to do!) as well as giving variety to presentational techniques. Taped material can be introduced – with the relevant pre-listening preparation – to focus attention on particular phonological points. These can be isolated and drilled in whatever way the teacher feels best.

2.8 Applications

Let's look at how a few of these techniques may be applied in the classroom:

The class is a beginner/elementary one. The objective is to teach the intonation patterns associated with simple choices (e.g. "Would you like this one or that one?").

The teacher introduces the lesson by saying that the topic will be 'choices' and checks that the learners are clear what he means. He uses a covert presentational technique (contextualised rather than grammatically oriented) that will lead on to exploiting the dialogue. The teacher asks a few questions such as: "Would you like the window open or closed?"/"I'm sorry, I've forgotten. Is your name Marta or Francesca?"

The teacher now introduces a dialogue which takes place in a shop between a shop assistant and a customer. He gives a brief outline of the content and pre-teaches some lexis – e.g. 'instant' 'ground' etc.

Shop assistant: Can I help you?

Customer: Yes. I'd like some coffee, please.

Shop assistant: Certainly. Would you like instant coffee or ground coffee?

Customer: Ground, please. Oh, and some chocolate.

Shop assistant: Right. Milk chocolate or plain chocolate? etc.

The teacher plays the tape through twice so that the learners are more or less familiar with the material. He asks them to listen out for the way that the shop assistant asks her questions. The focus is now upon the teaching point and the teacher plays the tape again, this time pausing after each of the questions. The class repeats chorally what they hear. After enough choral work to ensure that the learners are comfortable, individuals mimic the pattern.

The teacher writes one of the sentences up on the board:

Milk chocolate or plain chocolate?

The learners repeat it. The teacher draws direct attention to the intonation pattern by slightly exaggerating the tones. He raises his hand for a rising tone and lowers it for the falling tone. He then marks the sentence thus:

'Milk chocolate or `plain chocolate?

whilst emphasising the two nuclei and their tones. The class then repeats the pattern with the other choices from the dialogue. The teacher points out and demonstrates that the answer to the question has a fall:

`Milk chocolate, please.

Some further practice ensues and the teacher gets the learners to ask and answer questions themselves. Some initial prompts are given – e.g. Do you like classical music or pop music?

At first the teacher directs this by asking learners at random various general questions. Pair work follows where the learners ask each other 'two-choice' questions of their own making. This activity lasts some ten to fifteen minutes, during which the teacher monitors and helps the pairs. The teacher then draws the lesson to a close by getting the learners to ask him some 'two-choice' questions to check that they have grasped the intonation pattern.

2.9 Summary

In this chapter we have considered in broad terms some of the major aspects of suprasegmental phonology.

They have been:

- the syllable

- word-stress

- contrastive stress

- stress-timing

- intonation – including a discussion of intonation groups

In the applications section we have looked at:

- some systems for indicating stress and intonation

- exploiting a dialogue for phonological purposes

2.10 Key to the exercises

Ex. 1

one (1)	seven (2)	inspection (3)
introspection (4)	television (4)	cat (1)
nomad (2)	commercialisation (6)	psychiatry (4)

Ex. 2

<u>e</u>ven	<u>ru</u>gged	<u>pro</u>test (NOUN)	<u>peo</u>ple
		Or pro<u>test</u> (VERB)	
sup<u>port</u>	<u>pa</u>rent	app<u>eal</u>	<u>kid</u>nap

Ex. 3

What's your <u>name?</u>   Is it time to <u>go?</u>

How do you <u>do?</u>   Can I come <u>in?</u>

Would you like some <u>tea?</u>   What would you like to <u>drink?</u>

Chapter Three

Word stress and the syllable

What this chapter includes

3.1 Brief introduction

As we have seen, stress is an important factor in the phonological make-up of a word. When said in isolation, all words have stress – or to be more precise, a stressed syllable. Some words may lose stress when uttered in connected speech (in particular, words which have a grammatical function). This will be dealt with in the following chapter, but to get an idea of how stress affects the 'shape' of a word, try saying 'an' in isolation, and then in the sentence:

Can I have an apple?

Compare the way the two realisations of 'an' are pronounced. There is a difference between the production and quality of 'an' in the sentence and 'an' spoken in isolation. This is because in the sentence the 'an' does not have stress (normally at least) whereas 'an' spoken in isolation naturally does. What exactly does distinguish them, then?

3.2 Stress

There seems to be no single factor which determines stress. It is generated by a combination of loudness, length of syllable, pitch and muscular energy. The 'an' spoken in the sentence above, for example, requires less muscular energy than does the 'an' spoken in isolation. The sentence- 'an' vowel sound is a good deal more 'relaxed' and the cheeks and lips are by no means as tensed. Try contrasting the two varieties again to get an idea of this.

That this is a regular occurrence may be further demonstrated by the sentence:

I can open a can of beans.

Here the first 'can' differs in its value to the second in terms of the factors we mentioned above. It is less strident. However, in isolation 'can' (ability) and 'can' (the container) are identical. The difference is due to stress.

In simplified terms we can say that this stress will 'strengthen' a syllable, whilst lack of stress will make it less strong.

3.3 Word stress and word shape

In 3.2 we were considering monosyllabic words – those with just one syllable. But of course the majority of English words are not of this type. They have two or more syllables, and the distribution of stress within such words is a very significant factor in their realisation.

As we saw above, lack of stress tends to lead to less audible prominence for a syllable. Unstressed syllables are not, then, so noticeable as stressed ones. In the noun 'subject' (as in 'a British subject' or 'a school subject') the stress falls on the first syllable and this, then, stands out more than the second syllable. Compare this to the verb 'subject' (as in 'to subject to cross-examination'). With the verb, it is the second syllable that has the stress and that consequently stands out. Notice, too, that the vowel sound in the first syllable of the verb is rather different to the vowel sound in the first syllable of the noun. Just as we saw with function words, the fact that a syllable does not have stress leads to it being somewhat 'weakened'.

Word stress is a fundamental feature of di- and polysyllabic words (where di- refers to two syllables and poly- to three or more syllables) and is a key factor in decoding meaning. Mother-tongue speakers of English acquire a natural 'feel' for the phonological shape of words as they acquire the broader language system as a whole. For non-native learners of English, though, the seeming chaos (and, indeed, it may be just that!) of where stress falls in various words can be very daunting.

Consider the nonsense word:

Configulization

Where to you put the stress? Try saying it to yourself once or twice. You will almost certainly find that the most prominent syllable will be the penultimate one. The reason for this is that the suffix '-ation', as it were, grabs the stress for itself. Try saying some real words that further underline this:

nationalise   -   nationalisation (stress moves from first syllable)

organise   -   organisation (stress moves from first syllable)

Americanise   -   Americanisation (stress moves from second syllable)

compartmentalise -   compartmentalisation (stress moves from third syllable)

The most prominent syllable in the 'action' nouns is always the penultimate one.

Of course, mother-tongue speakers of English do not consciously carry around with them the rule: suffix '-ation' = penultimate syllabic stress! The operation takes place at a subconscious level. It is a rule which we develop a feel for, due to constant exposure (and probably some internal blue-print for the language). ESOL learners, however, do not have this same 'feel' and, hence, cannot readily predict where stress will or will not come in a given word. The problem is that placing the stress in the wrong place can lead to incomprehension and certainly this is something that ESOL learners find. Mother-tongue speakers can fail to recognise even the most everyday word if a learner places the stress incorrectly. Even at relatively advanced levels, learners still have to contend with this problem. Teachers, therefore, need to be sensitive to this aspect of 'learner talk'. It is all too easy in the classroom to miss or misinterpret what a learner is saying simply on the grounds of the stress being put in the wrong place. Some tolerance will be necessary, and encouragement should be given, for learners to feel that the problem can be tackled. However, such tolerance does need to be coloured by an awareness of the relative communicative goals that we have. Mother-tongue speakers outside the classroom rarely have the facility to decode learners' discourse as adeptly as ESOL teachers, who gradually develop an ear for it. At the end of the day, what we are looking for in our learners is an ability to communicate relatively fluently (and hopefully also accurately!) with fully competent speakers in the world beyond the classroom.

The stress-defining item we considered above is by no means the only one. In English there are a number of word-endings that will determine where the stress will fall. It is worthwhile for English language teachers to familiarise themselves with these, since one way of dealing with word stress, as we will see in the applications section, is by analogy – i.e. eliciting where the stress will come in an unknown word by getting learners to consider the stress pattern of words they already know. This not only gives the learners some stepping stones through the sea of stress structures but also has the advantage of contextualising phonology rather than dealing with it on an ad hoc basis. Added to this is the fact that it is more likely that learners will better assimilate and remember things that they have 'discovered for themselves' than things they have merely been told by the teacher. It is not possible, within the confines of this work to list all such word-endings but there are a number of textbooks available that do so (e.g. Roach 1983, pp79-82). Just to take another couple of examples, though, consider words like 'monsoon', 'balloon', 'cartoon' where the '-oon' element always takes the stress. Similarly words ending '-ic' will usually have the second to last syllable stressed (like the '-ation' words above): 'scientific', 'horrific', 'honorific' etc. Such words as the last three and the '-ation' examples are said to have **penultimate** stress. When words are stressed on the third syllable from the end, as normally they are if they finish with '-logy' ('biology', 'criminology' etc) then they are said to have **antepenultimate** stress. It should, however, be borne in mind that such word-endings do not account for the majority of word-stress patterns in English and will serve only as an aid rather than a cure-all.

3.4   More about the syllable

In Chapter 2 we looked in broad terms at what a syllable is and established a working definition. Perhaps before progressing any further we might look a little further into what features a syllable in English has.

We can begin by considering the structure of the English syllable. This often causes problems for ESOL learners. Syllabic structures vary quite markedly from language to language. Some languages will not allow more than one consonant in initial position in a word/syllable (the link between these two is in fact quite significant as we shall see). Some will not permit two or more in final position – and so on. This obviously has implications when we come to teaching pronunciation in the ESOL classroom.

English has the potential to generate syllables with the formula:

$$(C3) \ V \ (C4)$$

where ( ) indicates optionality. This means that up to three consonant sounds may initiate a syllable (or, of course, by extension a word). Following the initial **consonant cluster** there will (ordinarily!) be a vowel sound. Finally there can be up to four consonant sounds in the termination stage of the syllable.

Let's take some examples of this:

split = CCCVC (or C3VC1)

cat = CVC

cats = CVCC

sixths = CVCCCC

It seems straightforward enough. Surely it can't be? Afraid so! If we formulate the structure for the monosyllabic word 'rights' we arrive at CVCC. That is one initial consonant sound, a vowel sound and then two consonant sounds in final position. If we **read** the word 'rights' it would **appear** that it has **four** consonant sounds in final position. However, when we **speak** the word it does, in fact have just two – a t-sound and an s-sound. Since phonetics and phonology deal with the way language sounds, rather than the way that it looks on paper, then this is the analysis we must stick to. Originally the word **consonant** referred to a sound type that involved partial or total blocking of the airstream when speaking. It has, though, also taken on the meaning of letters of the alphabet that are not vowels (in other words, in English at least, all the letters of the alphabet excepting a, e, i, o and u). In this book we use the word **consonant sound** to refer to the former, more narrow, meaning. Thus although 'rights' has the non-vowel letters 'gh' immediately following the vowel, they are not pronounced. The same is true of the word 'psalm', which has the structure CVC since neither the p or the l has any sound value (in English).

Another slight complication lies in the fact that some individual letters of the alphabet comprise two sounds in speech. The letter x is made up of a k-sound and an s-sound. Thus the word fox will have the structure CVCC. The letter q is often (though not always) realised as a combination of a k-sound and a w-sound. Hence the word 'quick' has the structure CCVC (note also that the alphabetic sequence 'ck' occurs in speech as a single consonant sound).

All this may seem a little puzzling at first, especially as most of us are used to examining words based on their written rather than their spoken form. It is something, nevertheless, that needs to be borne in mind and will be further developed in Chapter 7.

Some languages, as mentioned above, will not allow such combinations of consonant sounds (clusters) as these we have been looking at. For example Spanish and Italian learners tend to have trouble with some initial consonant clusters in English and insert a vowel sound where none would exist in a native English speaker's pronunciation. Speakers of Oriental languages tend to have a problem both with initial clusters and final ones – sometimes to the point of not pronouncing syllable-final consonant sounds at all, thus giving rise to potential ambiguity of meaning.

3.5　Splitting the syllable

Marking the boundary between syllables is done in a particular way. This is dictated by the combination of consonant sounds found at the end of one syllable and the beginning of the next. In other words the type of consonant cluster found in syllable–initial and syllable-final positions will have a direct bearing on how we perceive a word's structure.

In English the rule seems to be that if a word can be broken down into two or more phonological units (i.e. if it is di- or polysyllabic), then their boundaries will initiate and terminate with combinations of consonant sounds that are recognised as being possible in initial or final positions in full words.

So, for example, if we consider the word 'athlete' the boundary between the two syllables will come after the 'th' and before the 'l' i.e. 'ath | lete' (where | marks the boundary). 'athl | ete' is not possible since 'thl' is not a permissible final combination of consonant sounds in English. Similarly 'a | thlete' is no good since 'thl' does not occur in initial position in any English word. The same type of thing is true for 'abstract' which is divided: 'ab | stract', since 'bstr' is not found in word initial position, and neither are '-bst' or '-bstr' found in final position, (for some speakers the division 'abs | tract' may also occur).

When syllables split across a single consonant sound – for instance in the word 'wagon' – another operation takes place. Here the syllable containing the latter vowel sound will normally have the consonant as its onset. Hence 'wa | gon' not *'wag | on'. Thus, when we have just one consonant sound involved, it will naturally initiate a syllable.

Interestingly enough, this is translated into connected speech. Take the short phrase:

'I've no idea at all'

How do you say the last two words? The tendency is for them to split as if they were a single word rather than two separate ones. Hence 'a │ tall' instead of 'at │ all' (unless you were really 'spelling out' your message!). Here we say that the natural word boundary has been **suppressed**.

On the basis of the above we can summarise by saying that in the case of di- and poly-syllabic words the tendency will be for a syllable to be **open** to facilitate a consonant-initial following syllable.

For example:

mo │ ther
(open) + boundary + consonant (open)

mo │ thered
(open) + boundary + consonant (closed)

Of course, languages are not identical in their choice and use of consonant clusters in initial and final position and thus we should bear in mind that some learners will have problems not just with consonant clusters themselves but also with the division of syllables in English words.

 Ex. 1

Say where the boundaries come between the syllables in the following words:

Examples: a │ fford   spe │ cial   me │ cha │ nic

pencil   penny   seven

seventeen   hurry   paper

advise   zephyr   video

In some cases there is an option as to where the boundary can come, for example in the word 'extra' (the x = ks as we saw above), the boundary could be:

ek | stra   or   eks | tra

and native speakers tend to use either possibility arbitrarily (this is known as free variation).

3.6   Primary and secondary stress

So far we have been concerned only with the single most prominent syllable in a word. This is fine as far as monosyllabic, and most disyllabic, words are concerned. But with polysyllabic words we need to go a little further. If we take, for instance, the word 'organisation' we find that the most prominent syllable is the penultimate one. It is an '-ation' type noun. However, the first syllable also stands out a little too. It is certainly more prominent that the second, third and fifth syllables even though it is relatively weaker than the fourth. This brings us to primary and secondary stress. In cases where we can detect another 'strongish' syllable as well as the most prominent one, we can distinguish them by saying that the former has secondary stress and the latter primary stress. Thus in 'organisation', the penultimate syllable carries primary stress and the initial syllable carries secondary stress. We might represent this diagrammatically as:

organisation

where the peaks indicate the 'amount of attention' that a syllable receives.

3.7 Applications

Whilst monitoring pair work during an upper-intermediate lesson dealing with ways of giving and accepting advice, the teacher notices that quite a few of the learners are having a problem with one of the words in the pattern dialogue that has been given out. Rather than stopping the lesson there and then to deal with it, and hence bringing that stage of the lesson to a premature end, the teacher makes a note of the problem. During the feedback that follows the end of the pairwork the teacher elicits from the learners the 'problem word'. Some of the learners are pronouncing 'combination' with stress on the second syllable, thus producing the vowel sound in a manner identical to that in 'com<u>bine</u>'. Other students are producing the correct stress pattern. The teacher asks which pronunciation is correct. Puzzled expressions reply. The teacher then elicits other words that the students are already familiar with which highlight the appropriate pattern of word stress. In doing this he also tries to maintain a focus on the functional objective of the lesson. He asks the students what advice they would give to someone coming to the U.K. to learn English. One of the replies inevitably raises the question of finding somewhere to live. The teacher exploits this idea by asking what specific advice the students might give regarding this. One of the learners suggests going to an accommodation office. The teacher writes the word 'accommodation' on the board. He then goes on to look for more instances of advice about choosing a suitable school to study at. The learners make a range of suggestions including the availability of examinations. The teacher writes up the word 'examination' on the board. He then asks where the stress comes in the two words on the board. The learners have no trouble in identifying it as falling on the second-to-last syllable. The teacher draws a box over the stressed syllable and then writes 'combination' beneath the two examples. He again asks where the learners think the stress comes in this word. Appreciating the general pattern, this time the learners all opt for the correct form. The teacher moves on to the next stage of the lesson.

3.8   Summary

In this Chapter we have looked at:

- word stress

- the structure of the syllable in English

- the form of boundaries between syllables

- some stress-defining word-endings in English

- primary and secondary stress

- a simple procedure for integrating phonology into a lesson.

3.9   Key to exercise 1

Ex. 1

pen | cil	pe | nny	se | ven
se | ven | teen	hu | rry	pa | per
ad | vise	ze | phyr	vi | de | o

Chapter Four

Sentence stress

What this chapter includes

4.1 Content and function words

It may seem odd for a chapter in a book on phonology to begin with a section on a subject which seems so clearly to be dealing with the grammatical organisation of the language. If it does, then let this serve as a reminder to you that the various compartments that linguists fit bits of the language into (syntax, phonology, lexis etc) are not really watertight at all. The syntax of a language may well, for example, be evidenced as much in its phonology as in its word order and this, indeed, is the case with English.

In Chapter 2 we introduced the idea of dividing the words of the language into content and function words and we suggested that, rather neatly, the language tended to mark the former in speech by stressing them and indicate the latter by not giving them stress. Just to recap, the situation is generally as follows:

GENERALLY STRESSED	GENERALLY NOT STRESSED
CONTENT WORDS (also called lexical words)	**FUNCTION WORDS** (also called structure words)
nouns e.g. book, Ray	(most) **determiners** e.g. some
(most) **verbs** e.g. go, speak	(most) **auxiliary verbs** e.g. am, can
adjectives e.g. pretty, blue	(most) **prepositions** e.g. for, to
adverbs e.g. always, nicely	(most) **conjunctions** e.g. but, as
	(most) **pronouns** e.g. us, she

The "(most)'s" in the lists above are a bit of a nuisance but we'll have to bear them in mind – in other words some of the generalisations we are going to make (and some we have already made) will have some important exceptions to them. Before we start looking at such details, however, here are a couple of exercises to help you practise separating words into these two broad categories.

Ex. 1

Just put a 'C' (for Content) or an 'F' for (Function) after each of the
following words.

doll ( )   his ( )   them ( )

evade ( )   must ( )   strange ( )

flimsy ( )   from ( )   with ( )

gloriously ( )   and ( )   opposite ( )

If you have a little trouble classifying some words in this way, don't worry – it's
normal if this is a new system of classification for you – just revise the word classes
in a modern descriptive grammar like Leech & Svartvik.

Ex. 2

Now try the same with some sentences:

1.   Put ( ) the ( ) flowers ( ) on ( ) the ( ) table ( ).

2.   The ( ) meeting ( ) ended ( ) with ( ) a ( ) vote ( ).

3.   The ( ) worst ( ) problem ( ) was ( ) the ( ) matter ( ) of ( ) status ( ).

4.   The ( ) effect ( ) of ( ) these ( ) gases ( ) is ( ) growing ( ) daily ( ).

5.   I ( ) had ( ) never ( ) spoken ( ) to ( ) her ( ) before ( ).

Before you check your classifications in this exercise listen to the tape and make
sure that your decisions about whether or not a word is a content word coincide with
the stress you can hear.

Now let's look at some of the exceptions to the rule. Remember the generalisation we are basing this on is that content words are stressed and function words generally are not.

4.1.1 Modal auxiliaries

In English the modal auxiliaries include: must, can, will, could, would, should, may, might, shall, ought. According to our rule these should be unstressed and routinely they are, but in ordinary affirmative sentences we can distinguish three different types of use of these modals. Because they give particularly clear examples we will look at 'must' and 'will' but what we will be saying is generally true for all of them.

Look at these example sentences and say them to yourself.

1. You must sign on the dotted line.

2. You **must** sign or I will kill you!

3. You must be crazy!

1a. He will be here in about fifteen minutes.

2a. He **will** be here despite the enormous difficulties!

3a. The dog will do such awful things just when the vicar is trying to drink his tea!

In sentences 1 and 1a we have the modal being used quite normally. In such a position it would normally be unstressed. In fact in 1a it would normally even contract with the preceding pronoun, which must be the ultimate in unstressing!

In sentences 2 and 2a we have the modals being used in an emphatic way and in such situations most native speakers who are not considering what they are doing analytically would stress the modal. We shall look at such exceptions as this more carefully in the next chapter.

In sentences 3 and 3a, however, note that something very special is happening to the modal. It has changed its meaning. If we say that the normal meaning of 'must' is connected with obligation then quite clearly the third sentence is not expressing some kind of obligation on someone to lose their sanity. Similarly 'will' is most usually used to express some kind of prediction about the future but in 3a we see it being used to express our dissatisfaction with the dog's **past** behaviour. In these two sentences it is virtually obligatory to stress the modal and this seems to be the way that native speakers signal phonologically that they are using a modal in a secondary rather than a primary sense.

Thus with the modals there seems to be a close connection between stress and meaning which can be summarised as:

normal meaning + normal situation = probably unstressed

normal meaning + emphatic situation = probably stressed

special meaning = almost inevitably stressed.

4.1.2   Auxiliaries in negative and interrogative utterances

You may have noticed that all the examples up to now have been affirmative. This is not an accident and in the following section we must look at what happens when we make a sentence with an auxiliary negative or use an auxiliary in a question. In this section we need to add the primary auxiliaries 'be' and 'have' together with the dummy operator 'do' to the list of modal auxiliaries that we had before.

(a)   negative utterances

There are various ways to make an utterance negative in English. By adding words like 'never', 'seldom' or 'rarely' to an utterance it becomes negative but these words do not seem to affect sentence stress very much. The most common marker of negativeness – 'not', on the other hand, does. Almost inevitably when 'not' is used to make a sentence negative, the auxiliary with which it is associated gains stress. Try saying the following sentences and test for yourself the stress that you give to the auxiliary:

I must get up earlier.

I mustn't get up earlier.

You should notice that the first one has two possible stress patterns depending on whether or not we wish to make 'must' emphatic, whereas the second sentence offers us no such alternative – the word 'mustn't' is stressed whether we like it or not.

(b)   interrogative utterances

There are various ways of making a question in English but here we are only concerned with polar questions (often, rather helpfully, called Yes/No questions because of the kind of answer they demand, e.g. "Do you like Brahms?", "Can you swim?" etc (these are termed polar questions because of the yes/no polarity of response). Other kinds of question in English do not seem to have a significant effect on sentence stress.

In polar questions we seem to have the option of adding stress to the auxiliary or not without affecting meaning. Compare:

You have finished.

with   Have you finished?

In the first sentence, spoken normally without any special emphasis, you should have no choice but to pronounce 'have' without stress. In the second you should find two ways of pronouncing 'have' which do not have any impact on the actual meaning of the question, though you may feel that certain circumstances may make one pronunciation more likely than the other.

4.1.3 Determiners, prepositions, conjunctions and pronouns which have more than one syllable

There are many words in English that fall into the above category – i.e. they are function words but they are polysyllabic and because of this they behave rather differently from their monosyllabic counterparts.

Here are some examples:-

determiners:	several, many
prepositions:	about, between
conjunctions:	whereas, although
pronouns:	themselves, someone

All such words carry stress and in this respect seem similar in sentences to content words.

Test this out for yourself by saying the following two sentences.

I've got some bananas.

I've got several bananas.

Do you notice the difference in rhythm of the two sentences caused by the extra stress that the second sentence has got?

4.2 The regular incidence of stress in English sentences

When native speakers of English produce sentences they have a tendency towards speaking rhythmically. (This is probably a natural tendency in all languages but as we shall see it has some important side-effects in English.)

The rhythm that English imposes on speakers seems to be based on the incidence of stressed syllables. This is not to say, of course, that all native speakers produce sentences with a 'tum ti ta' sort of regular rhythm – there are lots of opportunities and reasons for breaking the rhythm and it is only in special circumstances (strictly metrical poetry or rapping, for example) that we allow the underlying rhythm of the language to override other considerations.

Thus typical sentences like the following:-

There's a book on the shelf that you really ought to read.

and

The coach will stop in Hull and Leeds and York.

can easily be said without any kind of pause and are long enough stretches of speech for the rhythm to become quite clear – so clear, in fact, that if you say them repeatedly you will probably find yourself lapsing into a rather 'sing-songy' exaggerated rhythm.

This regular incidence of rhythm, then, is regular in the sense of fitting regularly into the time that passes as the sentences are said. It is not a regular feature in a more mechanistic sense (i.e. it doesn't, other than accidentally, fall on every second or third etc syllable).

4.3   Stress-timing

How long does it take to say a sentence in English?

We all expect questions like that in material like this to be disguising some sort of trap but the obvious and perfectly reasonable answer would be: "It depends how long the sentence is – longer sentences will take longer to say than shorter sentences".

If, for the moment we accept that this answer is all right the next question must be:- How do we measure the length of a sentence? Remember we're concerned here with pronunciation not writing so we can't provide answers like "you count the number of letters". We know that spelling can be a fairly unreliable indicator of pronunciation. Nor can we suggest counting the number of words since these vary quite dramatically in length themselves (function words and content words again).

Most people would agree that the most reliable indicator of the approximate length of a sentence is the number of syllables it contains.

Now let's try an informal experiment. If you've got a watch with a second hand try saying the following two sentences and measuring how long it takes you to say each of them. Do rehearse them first if it helps you to feel more comfortable and try to say them in as normal and relaxed a way as possible.

1 **Love makes the world go round yet hatred makes it grind to a halt.**

   Approximate time ………….. seconds.

2 **There's a book you'll appreciate at the bottom of the pile next to the one that my brother gave me on Saturday night.**

   Approximate time ………….. seconds.

Most people seem to take somewhere between 5 and 6 seconds to say either sentence with sentence 2 proving marginally longer, but only marginally. Yet sentence 2 contains 30 syllables and sentence 1, 15. If the number of syllables determined the duration of a sentence we could reasonably expect the second sentence to take twice as long as the first.

What we can conclude from all this is that the duration of a sentence in English does not depend on the number of syllables – it depends on something else. In the case of our two sentences that 'something else' must be more or less the same in the two sentences.

If we look at the two sentences again and count not the syllables but the **stressed syllables** we should discover what the two sentences have in common which makes them more or less equal in duration.

```
        1   2         3   4   5   6 7      8         9           10
```
1   **Love makes the world go round yet hatred makes it grind to a halt.**

```
        1              2              3              4   5          6
```
2   **There's a book you'll appreciate at the bottom of the pile next to the one**

```
        7       8          9          10
```
that my brother gave me on Saturday night.

Here then is a general principle of the pronunciation of English. It is not mysterious or complicated but it is part of the subconscious command all native speakers have of their own language. In more technical language we have been saying that English is a stress-timed language. So is Russian and some linguists claim that Brazilian Portuguese may also be stress-timed. Most languages, however, seem to be syllable-timed. That means that all the syllables – stressed or unstressed – in a sentence count towards the duration of the sentence. French is a good example of a syllable-timed language. French speakers of English with an incomplete mastery of our phonology may transfer their own syllable-timing to English and consequently sound very 'French' and similarly Edward Heath (if you've every heard him giving a speech in French) is a good example of someone doing the reverse. Many English people feel that rapidly spoken French reminds them of the sound of a machine gun (c.f. 2.4 and the example from Wilfred Owen). By the same token English must sound like Morse code to speakers of French.

Linguists are currently hotly disputing the validity of the stress-timed/syllable-timed distinction and when measured objectively there seems to be less evidence to support it than our ears report. Nevertheless in the context of TESOL it does seem to have pedagogic validity. As practising teachers of English we remain convinced that a reasonable amount of attention to this feature of the pronunciation of English produces enormous benefits both in our learners' pronunciation and in their ability to understand connected spoken English.

4.4   The phonological consequences of stress-timing

If, as we have said, English sentences have a fairly regular rhythm with beats falling on the stressed syllables and a more or less equal amount of time between them irrespective of the number of unstressed syllables between them, then something odd must happen to the unstressed syllables. Look at the sentence:

The bus came after we had been waiting for hours.

And now look at it with the stress indicated:

☐ ☐ ☐   ☐   ☐
The bus came after we had been waiting for hours.

If these stresses are more or less equally placed in time we can represent the interval between them as 'T'. Look what happens:

_T1 ☐ T2 ☐ T3 ☐ _____ T4 _____ ☐_T5 _____ ☐
The bus   came after we had been waiting for hours.

Remember that all those T's represent approximately the same amount of time measured from the end of one stressed syllable up to the beginning of the next.

The implication of this is, of course, that the amount of time at T2 is the same, for example, as the amount of time at T4. At T2, however, we are saying nothing as there is no intervening syllable between 'bus' and 'came' but at T4 we have to say '-ter we had been-'. How can we say four syllables in the amount of time we need to say none?

The language copes with this dilemma by ruthlessly compressing unstressed syllables. The most obvious way that this happens is apparent in the vowel sounds of unstressed words in connected speech. In other words we dramatically change the pronunciation of words in order to shorten them when compressing them between stressed syllables.

With many function words there is a sharp contrast between the way we pronounce them in isolation – their citation form – and the way we pronounce them in connected speech – often referred to as their weak form. (Please note that this term 'weak form' has unfortunate connotations. Do not allow yourself to imagine that for every weak form there is a strong form which would really be better. Rather, think of these weak forms as the normal form of the word – strong forms, when they exist, are reserved for special purposes in speech.)

Now look again at our sentence above and notice the vowel sounds in the unstressed words. (Remember to say the sentence in as normal a way as possible). You should have noticed that the unstressed words and parts of words in fact have only two different vowel sounds between them. They are:

the   we

(af)ter   been

had   (wait)ing

for

As we shall see more systematically later, these two sounds are represented in phonemic transcription by the symbols /ə/ and /ɪ/ respectively. The first one is particularly important in English and because it is difficult to pronounce accurately in isolation it has the unique distinction amongst the phonemes of English of having a name. It is named after a letter of the Hebrew alphabet, schwa (sometimes spelt shwa) and that is how we will refer to it from now on. Don't worry, by the way, if terms like phonemic transcription and phoneme are obscure at the moment. Be prepared to review these pages after you have read the later chapters on transcription.

The most important thing to notice is that though English has a lot of vowel sounds available generally, the language only uses the full range (minus schwa) in the stressed syllables of words in sentences. Thus the major phonological consequence of inter-stress compression is that a relatively restricted set of vowel sounds is available for unstressed syllables (predominantly schwa and /ɪ/).

4.5 Weak and strong forms

 Ex. 3

Here is an exercise to help you "tune into" weak and strong forms in the language. The following sentences are on the accompanying cassette or CD soundfile. What you have to do is listen to the featured word in each pair of sentences and decide which one is weak and which one is strong.

1. than

(a) She's better than I am.   WEAK/STRONG

(b) 'Than' comes between 'texture' and 'thanks' in my dictionary.
                                               WEAK/STRONG

2. there

(a) Is there any milk left?   WEAK/STRONG

(b) There's an old mill by the stream, they tell me.   WEAK/STRONG

3. of

(a) He's the only one I've ever heard of.   WEAK/STRONG

(b) A box of matches, please.   WEAK/STRONG

4. was

(a) Bobby Charlton was a marvellous striker.   WEAK/STRONG

(b) "Was there anything else, Sir?"   WEAK/STRONG

5.   can

(a)   "You-can-not-be-serious!"   WEAK/STRONG

(b)   I can see clearly now the rain has gone.   WEAK/STRONG

STOP THE TAPE/SOUNDFILE!

Before you listen to the rest, scan through them and predict whether they will be
weak or strong – then use the tape to confirm your predictions.

6.   and

(a)   I ate a full English breakfast, a five course lunch and a substantial dinner.

                                                                        WEAK/STRONG

(b)   I love fish and chips but I'm on a diet.   WEAK/STRONG

7.   from

(a)   Where's he coming from?   WEAK/STRONG

(b)   He came from a long line of aristocrats.   WEAK/STRONG

8.   us

(a)   Give us this day our daily bread …..   WEAK/STRONG

(b)   He didn't give it to us – he gave it to them.   WEAK/STRONG

9. **some**

(a) Some hope! WEAK/STRONG

(b) I'd love some cream on these strawberries. WEAK/STRONG

10. **to**

(a) He came to the party after all. WEAK/STRONG

(b) After the party he was some time coming to. WEAK/STRONG

NB Compiler's note: Exercises like this can very easily give the false impression that strong and weak forms are more or less equally distributed in the language. This is certainly not the case and it proved very difficult, in fact, to think up some reasonably realistic sounding examples containing strong forms.

4.6 Some problems students have in this area

Remember that a large proportion of our students originate from a language background that will have predisposed them to expect language to come to them in a syllable-timed form. The frequent compression of function words – the ones they need to perceive in order to get the grammatical structure of messages – may lead them to find stretches of spoken language quite unintelligible. Plenty of exposure to normal speech would probably help our learners to overcome this problem quite easily, were it not for a number of other factors which are common in the English learning experience of many of our students. These are:

i Early exposure to written forms rather than speech. There are no hints in written English about the relative stressing of different words and anyone who looks at a lot of written English but does not hear too much of it can be forgiven for assuming that equal value is given to all of the words in speech just as it is in writing.

ii   To make matters a little worse it is a fact of life that, for most learners of most foreign languages in most countries, the economics of mass education mean that most of the foreign language they are exposed to will be in the written form. Expensive though they may be, books are still currently for the majority of the world's learners of English, cheaper and more readily available than native or very competent speakers, tape recorders, CD ROMs, the Net, tape libraries and language laboratories.

iii   A further complication stems from the conviction (quite wrong, of course) that most of us share, that somehow the written form of the language is superior to the spoken one. Most of us feel instinctively that it is the written form of the language that preserves its most valuable features and that speech is merely an imperfect reflection of the norms established in writing. A moment's reflection will, of course, convince us otherwise. The majority of the world's languages still have no normally written form, yet are fully evolved, sophisticated and rule-governed linguistic systems for all that. No-one knows for sure how long the human race has had and used languages but what we can be sure of is that even the earliest written systems represent a very recent innovation on the timescale of the evolution of languages. The evidence of children acquiring their own mother tongue simply adds to this in that they master the grammatical system of their language and a significant proportion of its vocabulary some time before they begin to discover what may be the relatively unsystematic (at least as far as English is concerned) conventions of its writing.

iv   There is a further (often equally erroneous) conviction that many foreign learners share, that their own language is 'phonetic'. This nonsensical description usually seems to mean that they believe that there is a one-to-one relationship between the letters of their alphabet and the sounds of their language. From such a conviction springs the belief that the written system of a language will be a reliable indicator of its phonology. Whether or not this may be true of the language of a particular foreign student, you can well imagine that to transfer such a principle to English is dynamite!

v   Finally, there is evidence that during the acquisition of foreign and second languages students go through phases where they attempt subconsciously to strip the target language of those forms and details (third person singular –s, for example) which seem, to them, to be redundant. This is a complicated process

59

both to describe and to account for but suffice it to say that this process of redundancy reduction operates on the function word system – the unstressed words – and is one more impediment to their rapid and successful acquisition, their perception and their production.

4.7 Some steps teachers need to take

One of the major phonological problems that our learners present to us, then, is the overstressing of what should be unstressed words and syllables, especially in connected speech. This problem is linked in a complex way with their expectations of how the language **should** sound and a vicious circle ensures that it can then contribute actively to reducing their listening efficiency. The link, then, between listening and speaking is a complex interactive one – it is often very difficult to identify with any confidence what is cause and what is effect.

One thing, however, is certain. We cannot rely on weak listening skills to remedy weak pronunciation skills. In other words simply being exposed to accurate phonology does not lead in any rapid or predictable way to accurate production of that phonology.

There are two important implications to this state of affairs. Firstly we have to help our students in ways over and above simply giving them good models but secondly we must make sure that the models we give them **are** good, since obviously, exposure to bad models is going to be less beneficial than exposure to good ones.

Help other than aural help is likely to be visual and thus, ironically, we will frequently need to enlist the help of the blackboard, the overhead projector, wall charts etc in the struggle to sort out phonological problems. Our own experience has demonstrated time and again that students can be helped immensely with suprasegmental pronunciation by being allowed to **see** it as well as hear it(work in the area of Multiple Intelligences Theory would seem to support this). We have already discussed in the applications section of Chapter Two, various ways of representing stress and rhythm visually.

The question of consistently giving good models is a tricky one. This is one small but important area where teachers of English to Speakers of Other Languages actually need to distort their normal speech patterns in order to assist their learners. Since such an idea apparently runs counter to all accepted good practice let us explain carefully what we mean.

We have established already that words in English fall into one of two categories – either content or function words. We have also established that what distinguishes these two categories phonologically is that function words, unlike content words, present us frequently with a choice between a strong (or stressed) and weak (or unstressed) form.

Let us now remind ourselves that all of this holds true when we are talking about connected speech. But what happens if we **cite** a word in isolation – not in a sentence? Bear in mind that in a language class of all places citing words is a regular and natural event. Outside language classes it probably only happens regularly around Scrabble boards.

What happens is simple – in the case of content words – nothing at all. The citation form of such words coincides with the natural form quite closely so that the citation form will serve as a good model for the use of the word in connected speech.

In the case of function words, however, we have a problem. In almost every case the citation form of a function word coincides with the strong form – not the weak one.

In other words if we teachers cite a function word normally we will be presenting a model of that word which corresponds to its minority usage and we will be doing nothing to model its majority use.

There are two consequences of this. Firstly the students are exposed to fewer examples of the unstressed forms and secondly they may learn from us to put the stressed form into unstressed positions. A typical classroom exchange might look or rather sound like this:-

STUDENT: *I saw Queen on television.

TEACHER: No, Abdul, **the** Queen on **the** television – say it again.

STUDENT: * I saw **the** Queen on **the** television.

TEACHER: Good.

What the teacher has done is to encourage the student to exchange one error (the omission of the articles – or at least the first one) for another (the overstressing of them). The student's second sentence may look better on paper but the first one is arguably closer to being phonologically acceptable.

So how do we help students in such circumstances? As we said before a visual aid may solve the problem. Quickly writing on the board

I saw _____ Queen on _____ television

may elicit the articles from the student who quite possibly 'knows' that articles are more or less necessary in these positions. But failing that we may have to resort to citing the missing words and this is where a little distortion is for once valid. We need to be able to cite them in their unstressed form. At first doing so seems quite strange (though not particularly to our students) but it is well worth it to persevere in acquiring this valuable teaching skill.

Here is a list of words which routinely have an unstressed form – it is not an exhaustive list. Just for practice try citing the words without stress:

there (as in there's, there are etc)		the
am	an	or
are	must	rom
was	can	o
were	but	hem

have	has		ad

that (as in 'the boat that I row')   than

us	as

There are many more and as an exercise in familiarising yourself with the phonology of English it is well worthwhile adding to this list as you notice some of the others.

4.8   Applications

4.8.1   Jazz chants

The class consists of 25 children of late primary age (10-11). Their English is already at an intermediate level. The teacher has divided the class into two groups – boys on one side and girls on the other.

She has prepared an acetate for the OHP with the following chant on it:

GIRLS: Come on boys.
Please be quiet!

BOYS: We are quiet.
You're the noisy ones.

GIRLS: No we're not.
We're always good.

BOYS: Nonsense, girls.
We're always better.

She switches on the OHP but has the acetate masked with a sheet of paper so that she can focus on one line at a time. She does so and gets the appropriate group to practise until as a chorus they are producing the utterance both with acceptable rhythm and together. After getting to the last line she lets them run through the chant as a whole.

She now puts on an acetate with the same chant but with some words missing and the class choruses out their parts again once or twice. A further acetate with still fewer words follows (obviously overlays on the OHP would do as well for this).

After a few more run-throughs she is able to switch off the OHP while the class continue chanting.

****

Jazz chants are a very flexible medium. Clearly their topic does not have to be even mildly aggressive or divisive as is this one. Longer or shorter utterances can be employed – the themes can be topical, serious or amusing and they can be used with adult learners as effectively as with children. There is something quite attractive about choral speaking even in those cultures (like ours) where it is an unusual activity. Above all, the activity seems to help learners to internalise stress and rhythm patterns. For further ideas see <u>Jazz Chants</u> by Carolyn Graham.

4.8.2 Student-led dictations

The authors first read about this simple way of reversing roles in a dictation procedure in Seth Lindstromberg's 'Recipes for Language Teachers'.

It amounts to nothing more dramatic than the students dictating a passage to the teacher instead of the other way round. The teacher writes the dictation on the board. If this is done with children the teacher can role-play a robot, with adults the teacher simply has to be rigorously literal. Either way what goes on the board must be exactly what the students say. As the students, for example, struggle to say the word 'for' but find the teacher repeatedly writing it on the board as 'four' they are helped to understand that there is really a phonological point to the unstressing of function words. A useful spin-off of this procedure is that students seem to gain insights into the limitations of the help provided by the written form of the language when it comes to speaking it.

4.9 Summary

In this chapter we have

- tried to identify those words which are routinely stressed in English and those which are routinely unstressed.

- tried to identify the conditions which determine whether a word is stressed or unstressed when the language allows us a choice.

- noted that connected speech in English tends to be stress-timed whereas most other languages tend to be syllable-timed.

- noted the consequences of stress-timing on the pronunciation of connected speech.

- practised distinguishing between weak and strong forms in context.

- looked at some of the difficulties these features create for foreign learners of English.

- briefly considered some of the implications of this for teachers' classroom language.

- looked at Jazz chants and reversed dictations as classroom devices for focusing on and generating productive practice in sentence stress.

4.10   Key to the exercises

Ex. 1

doll (C)	his (F)	them (F)
evade (C)	must (F)	strange (C)
flimsy (C)	from (F)	with (F)
gloriously (C)	and (F)	opposite (F)

Ex. 2

1   Put (C) the (F) flowers (C) on (F) the (F) table (C) .

2   The (F) meeting (C) ended (C) with (F) a (F) vote (C) .

3   The (F) worst (C) problem (C) was (F) the (F) matter (C) of (F) status (C) .

4   The (F) effect (C) of (F) these (F) gases (C) is (F) growing (C) daily (C) .

5   I (F) had (F) never (F) spoken (C) to (F) her (F) before (C) .

Ex 3

1   **than**

   a   She's better than I am.   WEAK

   b   'Than' comes between 'texture' and 'thanks' in my
      dictionary.   STRONG

2   there

    a   Is there any milk left?   WEAK

    b   There's an old mill by the stream, they tell me.   WEAK

3   of

    a   He's the only one I've ever heard of.   STRONG

    b   A box of matches, please.   WEAK

4   was

    a   Bobby Charlton was a marvellous striker.   WEAK

    b   "Was there anything else, Sir?"   STRONG

5   can

    a   "You-can-not-be-serious!"   STRONG

    b   I can see clearly now the rain has gone.   WEAK

6   and

    a   I ate a full English breakfast, a five course lunch and a
         substantial dinner.   STRONG

    b   I love fish and chips but I'm on a diet.   WEAK

7   from

    a   Where's he coming from?   STRONG

    b   He came from a long line of aristocrats.   WEAK

8　**us**

    a   Give us this day our daily bread ...   WEAK
    b   He didn't give it to us – he gave it to them.   STRONG

9　**some**

    a   Some hope!   STRONG
    b   I'd love some cream on these strawberries.   WEAK

10　**to**

    a   He came to the party after all.   WEAK
    b   After the party he was some time coming to.   STRONG

Chapter Five

Major intonation patterns

What this chapter includes

5.1   A brief introduction

We have already considered some of the principles involved in intonation – such things as sentence stress, nuclear stress, nuclear tones, intonation groups. In this chapter we will be looking in more detail at the mechanics of intonation and focusing, in particular, on some of the most important intonation patterns in English. The next chapter will deal with how stress, a phenomenon intimately connected with intonation, can directly and very markedly affect meaning in discourse. But in order to fully appreciate this, we must first get a general idea of how intonation patterns are realised.

5.2   Analysing the intonation group

Let's begin by revising some of the points we touched upon in Chapter 2. Take the sentence:

It was a crazy thing to get involved in.

This would normally have '-volved' as the nuclear stress if spoken in a 'neutral' manner – i.e. stressing only the act of 'getting' involved. The nuclear tone would therefore commence at this point. The direction of the tone will be downwards – a fall. In looking further we can distinguish the pre-head – any unstressed syllables that precede the first stressed syllable of the intonation group. Here the pre-head contains three syllables – notice they are all function words – 'it', 'was', and 'a'. The head begins with the first syllable of 'crazy' and stretches to the nuclear stress, thus ending on the first syllable of 'involved'. As we mentioned '-volved' takes nuclear stress and has a falling nuclear tone which stretches over two syllables here: '-volved' itself and 'in'. 'In', then, forms the tail (which, as you'll recall, is made up of any syllables which follow the nuclear stress in the same intonation group).

Now let's consider a related, but slightly different example:

John was crazy to get involved in such a thing.

Keeping the nuclear stress on '-volved-, here we can see that there is no pre-head. 'John' carries stress and therefore the intonation group begins with the head. The head here contains seven syllables. Notice, though, that the tail in this example consists of four syllables, '… in such a thing.' Again, we would normally expect a fall on '-volved'. But what happens to the pattern of pitch in the tail? In fact, what happens is that after the fall on the nuclear stress syllable, the tone 'levels off' and the pitch is even across the tail. In other words, the tail '… in such a thing' is spoken on a monotone. Practise this by isolating the last four syllables and humming them. If you then speak them, you should be able to detect their level tone, and repeating them end to end '… in such a thing, … in such a thing, … in such a thing' etc should demonstrate their monotony. Tag on an extra intonation group to the first and you may be able to detect a regular pattern, as in:

John was crazy to get involved in such a thing | in the first bloody place!

where 'first' carries the nuclear stress of the second intonation group and 'bloody place', as the tail, is spoken with low, level pitch.

This feature is indicative of the first pattern we will consider.

5.3   The four most important patterns

5.3.1   Falling intonation

The syllables contained in the tail which follow a simple fall are spoken with a level pitch.

This much is relatively easy to detect and classify. Turning our attention to the syllables in the head segment (or the pre-nuclear segment) we can detect a gradual, though punctuated, rise from 'John' up to 'in-'. However, though this is true of the example we are considering, such an approach to the nuclear stress may not always occur. Sometimes there may be a level pitch approach, sometimes a slight, gradual fall.

There are numerous works that detail such aspects of intonation, and, for the sake of brevity (and an acknowledgement that these works are, of course, more comprehensive than this particular book can be in this regard), we recommend that readers with a particular – and voracious! – appetite for the 'fine-print' of the subject consult one of these. O'Connor's 'Phonetics' (1973) is useful, as is Bolinger's 'Intonation and its Parts' (1985).

It is important not to get the pitch pattern in the pre-head and head sections confused with the communicatively more significant change in pitch that begins with the nuclear syllable. Again, probably the easiest way to sensitise yourself to this is by humming, rather than speaking, utterances. The marked change in tone, pitch and prominence at the nuclear syllable should be quite apparent. This is also a useful technique to practise with learners, especially at an elementary stage. One of the complications of coming to terms with any new language is the fact that several different things are happening at once and this makes initial perception, and therefore production, really quite tricky. If we strip away, as it were, the phonemes of a sentence and just concentrate on the rhythmic base of an utterance we can help our learners to perceive things more clearly. Superimposing the articulation of individual sounds on top of the underlying rhythm is a difficult task, but clearly one that learners need to master fairly quickly. Nobody is going to understand someone who just hums a language! However the value of this technique is in ear-training as much as production and it can go some way to highlight the sound pattern of English.

Both high and low falls have some degree of finality to them. This is not to suggest that they always signal the completion of discourse but they tend to imply statement-like information or 'one-way' information transfer. They can also seem neutral or matter-of-fact, even disinterested. However, Gimson (1980) does point out that between close friends, conversation may contain a lot of falling intonation patterns without seeming odd or impolite (as it would between acquaintances or strangers).

Low falls often signal boredom or lack of interest, though they are, too, a feature of some items of phatic communion. The distinction here is in the nature of the head: a high pitch head approach to the nucleus shows interest in a conversation, whilst a low pitch approach sounds matter-of-fact or bored.

5.3.2   Rising intonation

As well as simple falls, we can also have simply rises. Very often yes/no questions have this particular intonation pattern as in:

Do you take milk in your coffee?

where 'milk' has nuclear stress and '... in your coffee' forms the tail.

To get an idea of the contrast between rises and falls, read the following sequence out loud:

one, two, three, four, five.

On each of the first four items there will be a rise. Each constitutes a separate intonation group. With the completion of the sequence a falling nuclear tone is used. This actually shows that the sequence is complete. Rises, with regard to giving sequences, show that something else is coming up. The same is true of lists and also of constructs like the one we considered in Chapter Two, dealing with offering choices. In each case the item that closes or finishes the sequence, list or range of choices will have a fall, the others will have a rise.

It is, perhaps easier to detect rises than falls, because the syllables in the tail of an intonation group following the nuclear stress tend to continue the rise, rather than levelling out like those that follow a simple fall on the nuclear stress. So, for example, in the second sentence below, the nuclear stress is on 'where' and the rise continues quite noticeably over the following syllables:

A: They're going to Vladivostok.

B: **Where** are they going!!?

Other than this the same criteria apply for rises as for falls with regard to the nature of the syllable itself. Syllables with longer vowel sounds will have a rising tone that is more noticeable than syllables with short vowel sounds.

In simple rises and simple falls the movement of pitch in the nuclear and post-nuclear segment is in just one direction – either up or down. With rises, as we said, the movement is, perhaps, more noticeable than with falls, due to the upward tune continuing right across the syllables that follow the nuclear stress. However, nuclear tones can sometimes both rise and fall or vice versa. Such types of tone are called fall-rises and rise-falls. Let's take a look at fall-rises first.

73

5.3.3 The fall-rise

In a fall-rise, the nuclear tone that begins with the syllable that has nuclear stress first dips and then moves up in pitch. This type of tune is characteristic of turn-taking in conversation. Tones that end with a slight rise sound more friendly and inviting than simple falls. They signal that the conversation is not at an end and that another person's input is welcome. Simple rises, on the other hand, signal that the speaker wants to 'keep the floor' and that their 'turn' is not yet over.

This may explain, in some degree, why non-native speakers of English are sometimes said to sound 'rude' by native speakers. The subtle rises that follow a nuclear tone falling help to send out positive signals in terms of overall discourse. Falls and particularly high falls, by their nature, sound rather final and signal a break in discourse – either partial or complete. Learners from non-intonationally inclined languages are, quite understandably, likely to be unaware of such subtle nuances operating above the level of pure sounds and words. The word 'please' often is spoken with a fall-rise, as in:

A loaf of bread, please.

If uttered with just a fall the effect is somewhat 'demanding' in tone (in tone, see!). In German, for example, the equivalent to English please is 'bitte' but this is usually spoken with a simple fall. By literally transferring a German intonation pattern to English the effect is unlikely to be successful in conveying politeness.

Fall-rises can also signal mild amusement, puzzlement or surprise.

5.3.4 The rise-fall

Rise-falls may occur, too. These are slightly rare, though. Here we have a partial or slight rise in pitch followed by a medium or high fall. In each case the initial rise helps to draw attention to the fall that follows. They are often used to show sarcasm, irony or indignation and can be employed for comic effect, mostly to signal some kind of innuendo. The British comedian Frankie Howard was a notable deployer of such intonation patterns!

5.4   Applications

Interestingly, it seems to be the case that intonation lies squarely within the acquisition camp as regards coming to terms with English. It **appears** that intonation is subconsciously picked up rather that consciously learned. The key to this may well be the fact that while learners (or should they be acquirers?!) are focusing on structural, lexical and semantic features of the language, intonation quietly goes about establishing itself in a relatively painless way.

So long as the teacher provides a relatively authentic model, then we can be reasonably sure that learners will 'get to grips' with intonation and its parts. It is not all that necessary to start isolating discrete units of the system and draw particular attention to them. Indeed, many teachers of English (or any language for that matter!) feel quite understandably uncomfortable about presenting learners with specific points concerning the phonological system. As you have probably found from reading this chapter, it ain't all that simple! The best advice that can be given on this is: **don't worry!** As native speakers, or competent speakers of English as a foreign language, we can all operate the system perfectly well and with ease. We do it without thinking about it. This, then, will do. It will provide learners with the model and it will, even more importantly, provide it in context. So the ideal, perhaps slightly ironically, when teaching intonation is not to draw too much attention to it but simply get on with teaching whatever might be the target of any given lesson and speaking naturally.

One thing to watch, though, is the presentation of certain items, in particular function words, in this authentic fashion that we have been championing. (Although we mentioned this in the context of sentence stress in Chapter 4, it is certainly worth repeating the same idea now with the added focus of nuclear stress). It is very easy to fall into the trap of giving them unnatural stress just because we are pointing them out. Consider the present perfect tense. What is the formulaic constant of this particular structure? Answer: the auxiliary verb **have** plus the **past participle** of the lexical verb. Now ask yourself how the auxiliary verb is actually uttered in normal spoken language. You should notice that it is 'weak'. It is realised as a syllable that has a weak vowel (in fact schwa) at its centre. It may even reduce right down to a /v/ as in 'I've just seen Mary'. Very rarely would it be used in its strong form – the way we tend to say it in isolation. When uttered thus and therefore carrying stress it has emphatic value, as in 'I **have** seen Mary!!' (So stop contradicting me!, for example). The implication of such a realisation is outside the actual sentence itself. It is a matter of inference. Obviously learners of English need to come to terms with such a phenomenon, **but** when initially presenting structures that incorporate weak forms it is important to try to utter them as such. Again this takes practice and isn't as easy as it might seem. The reason for this is that because English has an intonational system that can use stress (in particular nuclear stress) to point out the significant item in a long line of items, when we are pointing out, say, the formulaic components of the present perfect tense, it is 'natural' to stress them. That is we would tend to say "Look! Look! **I** (pause) **HAVE** (pause) **SEEN** (pause) **Mary**." Fair enough, it gets over the importance of the formula, but what it doesn't do is provide learners with an authentic model. It doesn't indicate to learners the way we would **normally** say such a sentence. For learners coming from languages that don't operate an intonation system identical to ours (i.e. just about everybody!) there is no reason that they should be able to make a subjective judgement as to whether or not 'have' would or would not be stressed ordinarily. Why might they? What they **would** do is follow the model that the teacher has provided and <u>always</u> stress 'have'. This is one of the things that leads to misunderstanding when learners are talking to native speakers. Native speakers of English are not used to listening to language where everything is stressed. They can't then judge what is and is not important in a given utterance. Thus when presenting new items to learners (and subsequently too) it's best to aim to present them as they would actually be said (in the weak form) and not to lend special emphasis to them.

  Ex. 1

This exercise, which is on the accompanying cassette or CD Rom, provides you with a number of phrases. Play the tape as many times as you need to and write in the brackets after each intonation group what you think it is. Use the following labels:

FALL
RISE
FALL-RISE
RISE-FALL

When in doubt, try hard to listen only to the nuclear tone and the tail – try to ignore the head and pre-head.

1   What's your name? (   )

2   What's your name? (   )

3   Very interesting. (   )

4   Are you coming to the party? (   )

5   Three, (   ) six, (   ) five, (   ) nine, (   ) seven, (   ) eight. (   )

6   Charming (   )

7   I like Mr Smith. (   )

8   She went there on business. (   )

9   Do you speak Chinese? (   )

10 Open the window. (   )

11 Open the window. (   )

12 I wouldn't exactly call him handsome. (   )

13 But at least he's rich. (   )

14 Why on earth did you do that? (   )

15 I asked him where he came from. (   )

5.5 Summary

In this chapter we have:

- looked at ways of analysing intonation groups into pre-heads, heads, nuclear tones and tails

- identified the following major intonation patterns:

  1 falling intonation

  2 rising intonation

  3 the fall-rise

  4 the rise-fall

- considered the application of this knowledge in the classroom in terms of the need to control teacher language especially when presenting new items

- provided practice in the recognition of major intonation patterns

5.6 Key to exercise 1

1   What's your name? (FALL)

2   What's your name? (RISE)

3   Very interesting. (FALL)

4   Are you coming to the party? (RISE)

5   Three, (RISE) six, (RISE) five, (RISE) nine, (RISE) seven, (RISE) eight. (FALL)

6   Charming (RISE-FALL)

7   I like Mr Smith. (FALL-RISE)

8   She went there on business. (FALL)

9   Do you speak Chinese? (RISE)

10   Open the window. (FALL)

11   Open the window. (RISE)

12   I wouldn't exactly call him handsome. (FALL-RISE)

13   But at least he's rich. (FALL)

14   Why on earth did you do that? (FALL)

15   I asked him where he came from. (FALL)

Chapter Six

Special effects achieved with stress and nuclear stress

What this chapter includes

6.1 Introduction

The placement of nuclear stress in utterances is, as we have seen in Chapter Five, critical in determining the overall intonation contour of an utterance. More than that, however, in a language like English where there is generally little scope for altering the communicative effect of a given utterance by, for example, rearranging the word order, the placement of nuclear stress can have a profound effect on the meaning of an utterance.

In this chapter, then, we are going to look at how we manipulate stress in words and nuclear stress in longer utterances to affect meaning.

Please remember that when we talk about 'nuclear stress' in the sections that follow we are, to some extent, using this term as a kind of shorthand. The phenomenon that we are dealing with is a fairly complex bundle of acoustic components, including volume, duration and pitch. Despite its complexity it does seem to have psychological reality – i.e. native speakers (and as a rule, foreign learners) can identify it and thus locate it in utterances. Complaints such as "It wasn't so much what he said as the way that he said it" are commonplace testimony to our sensitivity towards the manipulation of nuclear stress. What such complaints really mean in rather more technical language is – "No-one could possibly take exception to the word order of his sentence, the choice of vocabulary etc, but he chose to impose a special and offensive meaning on it by shifting the nuclear stress to a position that was other than that one would normally predict in this sentence and this had repercussions on the overall intonation contour of the utterance".

6.2 Variability of word stress

We are going to deal with this phenomenon briefly at the beginning of this chapter because it really is not worth spending a lot of time on. It is a common topic in EFL coursebooks and manuals on pronunciation but probably only because it is easily identifiable – not because it is particularly common, important or even reliable as a feature of the pronunciation of native speakers. The phenomenon is most commonly observed amongst those words which when crossing word class boundaries shift their word stress. Thus a word like 'import' can be a noun or a verb. When the former, it is stressed on the first syllable, when the latter, it is usually (by now you should be hearing mental warning signals every time you read the word 'usually'!) stressed on the second syllable. Unfortunately for every word like 'import' that you can find in the language you will find a hundred examples of noun/verb items like 'feature' where there is no stress shift available.

It is even easy to find examples of words like 'import' in context where other stress considerations override the variable word stress – think, for example of a sentence like –

"Britain should be <u>ex</u>porting cars, not <u>im</u>porting them."

Here although 'importing' (and 'exporting' for that matter) is clearly a verb, it is stressed on the first not the second syllable for contrastive reasons. There seems to be some evidence that this feature of word class dependent word stress location is not a stable feature across the various varieties of English. Thus the fact that in British English we may usually distinguish between 'compound' (adjective or noun) and 'to compound' (verb) is no cast iron guarantee that American versions of English will do the same.

To summarise, then, this seems to be a rather insignificant backwater of the phonology of English, which, nevertheless, receives rather a lot of attention in published course materials. Our position as teachers should probably be to deal with it as and when it is brought to our learners' attention but not to go out of our way to draw their attention to it ourselves.

6.3   Nuclear stress at a syntactic level

If it is possible to talk of intonation and stress as two separate systems within the phonology of English (many would claim that these two features are so intimately connected that they are inseparable), then it is also possible to identify the nuclear stress in any intonation group as the point at which the two systems interact. This interaction – the coincidence of full stress with a substantial pitch movement – highlights a particular part of the utterance and gives it prominence. We have seen this mechanism in some detail in the preceding chapter and in the following section we are covering some of the same ground as in Chapter Five but with our interest focused on stress rather than intonation this time.

Rules are made to be broken. However one may feel about such a concept in life, there is much evidence of its validity in human communications systems and particularly in languages. In other words, one way that human beings exploit rule systems is by conventionally breaking them.

The flying of the Union Jack is an example. If you were a Scout or Guide, forgive me for pointing out that there is a correct way for this flag to be flown. Breaking the rule and flying the flag upside down is a distress signal. If, then, flying the flag the right way up is a communicative act because it adheres to a 'rule', turning it upside down ('breaking the rule' deliberately) adds an extra layer of meaning to that act. The fact that the rule is unknown to the majority of spectators simply means that this particular communicative act only has communicative value to a restricted group within the community.

In the rather more complex world of the phonology of English, we see a rather similar situation with the location of nuclear stress in an utterance. The 'rules' tell us that normally in English there is a high probability of the nuclear stress coinciding with the last stressed syllable of an intonation group. Thus, to shift it somewhere else will serve as a signal to the listener that extra meaning is being added to what is being said.

Look at the following sentences in Spanish and their word for word translations into English:

1	Mañana te lo daré.	Tomorrow to you it I will give.
2	To lo daré a ti mañana.	To you it I will give to you tomorrow.
3	Yo mismo te lo daré mañana.	I myself to you it I will give tomorrow.
4	Te lo daré – no te lo venderé – mañana.	To you it I will give – not to you it I will sell tomorrow.

The word for word translations are, of course, horrific but they illustrate well how Spanish uses syntactic devices to shift prominence around an utterance where

English deals with the same need phonologically. More appropriate translations of the four sentences, then, would be:

1   I'll give it to to<u>morr</u>ow.

2   I'll give it to <u>you</u> tomorrow.

3   <u>I'll</u> give it to you tomorrow.

4   I'll <u>give</u> it to you tomorrow.

In these examples the underlined syllable represents the nuclear stress.

A simple example like this demonstrates quite well how the exact meaning of an utterance in English is quite dependent on our capacity for manipulating the 'rules', and how powerfully this manipulation alters meaning.

6.4   Nuclear stress as an indicator of speaker intention

If we look at a sentence like:

A five year old could understand this.

and give it a nominal stress and intonation pattern, thus:

A five year old could under<u>stand</u> this.

we have a statement which is saying no more and no less than:-

"This (whatever 'this' is) is within the cognitive competence of a human child of five years."

A simple shift of nuclear stress, however, with its inevitable effect on the intonation contour of the whole utterance will give us a sentence like:

A <u>five</u> year old could understand this!

The intention of the utterance has changed radically. It has ceased to be an apparently objective statement of presumably verifiable fact and has become a shamelessly subjective criticism of either the listener(s) or a third party. It now seems to mean: "you/he/she/they is/are stupid in your/his/her/their lack of comprehension, which, as far as I am concerned, is at a level lower than that of a five year old child!".

This is a subtle area of native speaker manipulation of phonology and permits us to overlay seemingly neutral utterances with a wide range of (generally emotive) intentions, many of which are negative, such as irony, sarcasm, disapproval, aggression. Arguably we are reaching an area of phonology which is deeply subconscious in native speakers and for which a productive capacity is probably beyond the reasonable expectations of foreign learners other than the most advanced students of the language.

6.5   Implications for the classroom

It is worth giving some time and thought to this phenomenon as teachers of ESOL for one very good reason. There is some evidence (mostly, admittedly, anecdotal) to suggest that learners of English quite rapidly acquire insights into this system on a receptive level. The evidence comes from observation of classroom situations in which a totally new teacher with a particular class gains (or does not, as the case may be) rapport with the class. There are, of course, many very complicated factors involved in the establishment of rapport but a particularly important one may well be the closeness the teacher achieves when talking between speaker intention and the syntactic evidence. In other words the extent to which these two communicative levels in speech complement and reinforce each other rather than contradicting each other. Successful experienced ESOL teachers and those newcomers to the field who seem naturally to establish rapport rapidly, tend to match the syntactic form of their utterances predictably to the intentional placement of nuclear stress. It is as if, on entering an ESOL classroom, they temporarily suspend the facility for overlaying additional meaning through the manipulation of nuclear stress placement and thus manage to communicate with their students more directly and more efficiently.

This all sounds very complicated, doesn't it? So, let's look at a concrete example. Look at the following utterance:

"That was really very <u>good</u>, Mahmood!"

As this stands it is a straightforward example of teacher evaluation but can you see that by the simple expedient of shifting the nuclear stress and making the resultant adjustments to intonation we can express something very different. Thus:

<u>That</u> was really very good, Mahmood!"

We now have a sentence that actually means:

"Although, Mahmood, you are generally a pain in the neck, you have, on this particular occasion, actually managed to get something right!"

You may feel that this is an exaggerated interpretation but since this particular exasperated comment comes from one of my own lessons you'll have to take my word for it!

What happens in the ESOL classroom when teachers produce utterances of this kind is that students quickly recognise that many utterances from the teacher probably do not have their 'face value' – what students cannot easily do is assign such utterances their intended value. Thus after such an utterance is made, if the student has successfully decoded the utterance at a syntactic level the student knows:

1.   What the teacher apparently said.

2.   That the teacher did not mean what he/she apparently said.

The student probably does not know:

3.   What the teacher meant.

This is not a formula that readily enhances rapport between teacher and learners.

Many teachers experience no difficulty establishing rapport with their classes but cannot explain why this is the case – many teachers have difficulty establishing rapport with their classes and are equally, though more distressingly, at a loss to explain why this is. It is not our intention to overstate the case here and suggest that conscious control of the placement of nuclear stress is the key to popularity in the ESOL classroom but we offer the idea to those who are willing to accept this small self-discipline as a possible step in the right direction.

6.6 Nuclear stress employed for contrastive purposes

It is a very common phenomenon in English that we use nuclear stress to indicate to our listeners that we are making or implying a contrast. Consider, for example, utterances like:

"I like <u>Scotch</u> whisky but I'm not fond of <u>Ir</u>ish whisky."

The nuclear stress on 'Scotch' predisposes the listener to expect a contrast later in the utterance.

Consider also an utterance like:

"I like <u>Mrs</u> Smith ..."

In utterances like this the contrast is so restricted that the second element need only be implied.

The general procedure in English seems to be that if we want to make some contrastive point about an open class we have to be explicit and complete the utterance. If, on the other hand, we only plan to contrast a member of a closed class, the choices available to our listener(s) are often restricted enough for the message to be complete without actually saying the second element of contrast.

Similarly, even with open class items, if the preceding discourse (or even situational or cultural constraints) has sufficiently restricted available choices, the contrast can be dealt with purely phonologically and the second element becomes redundant –

e.g.
    A: "Do you like Brahms and Beethoven?"

    B: "I like Brahms ...."

Or

A: "Would you like a hot drink?"

B: "I'd love some tea ...."

For cultural reasons, here most native speaker listeners would supply an implied contrast with coffee rather than, say, skimmed Yak's milk or fermented cactus juice.

It is probably in the categories of closed class contrasts, e.g.

"I didn't do it ..."

and culturally restricted open class contrasts, e.g.

"If you're going to the chippie I'd love some <u>fish</u> ..."

that our learners need most help since the utterances concerned, decoded on a syntactic level, may well appear to be rather cryptic and language learners naturally do not have the same predictive powers as native speaker listeners.

6.7 Applications

As we saw in Chapter Five it is a little difficult to isolate large suprasegmental phonological phenomena so as to generate discrete practice of them in the classroom. Many authors have, however, tried to assist teachers in this area and notable among them is Helen Monfries whose little book <u>Oral Drills in Sentence Patterns</u> contains a lot of useful drill-type exercises. Certain reference grammars contain indications of neutral stress and intonation in example utterances in case you are ever in doubt about what you really normally say and grammars of this type such as <u>Active Grammar</u> by Bald et al can thus serve as a starting point for devising your own practice procedures.

In general, however, it is probably best to say that most of the matters dealt with in this and the preceding chapter will respond better to integrated rather than isolated treatment. Thus major intonation tunes and variations in the placement of nuclear stress should be dealt with as and when they naturally occur as a feature of a structure or function that the class is focusing on.

Given that these are matters that are normally below the level of conscious control in native speakers it can be argued reasonably that we cannot expect foreign learners to have a conscious control of them. Thus, though we may use visual aids like the board to indicate nuclear stress or movements of our arm to represent an intonation tune we should not expect such aids to be much more than psychological props for our learners.

The key issues here are:

1   (in the short term) can our learners successfully mimic a model?

2   (in the long term) can our learners consistently get this feature right after their initial mimicking success?

To this end a colleague who was particularly keen to cover this aspect of the language thoroughly would devote three or four minutes of lessons when new sentence patterns or realisations of functions were being introduced to the choral and individual repetition of marker sentences. For a term she transferred such marker sentences with graphic indications of stress and intonation to large strips of paper which were added incrementally to a wall display in the classroom. In this way she satisfied herself in the short term that a pattern has been mastered and in the long term maintained a reference and reminder facility in the classroom for those who were momentarily in doubt.

6.8 Summary

In this chapter we have looked at variable word stress and variable nuclear stress. The former we have suggested is relatively unimportant and unproductive as a teaching point. The latter we have considered as an important feature, noting how the shifting of prominence from one part of an utterance to another alters the message being given and, it is hoped, being received. We have seen how we manipulate nuclear stress to add special intentions to utterances and we have noted how as teachers using the target language as the language of instruction we must take care to monitor our communication with our classes in this respect.

Finally we have looked at the manipulation of nuclear stress for contrastive reasons and noted that we have a fairly rich system of contrastive stress and that learners probably need help when the meaning of messages depends more on phonological signals than on explicit syntax.

In other words we have:

- considered the variable placement of stress in words

- considered the variable placement of stress in sentences

- considered the implications of this for the transmission of meaning

- considered the implications of this for a teacher's classroom language

- looked at stress used contrastively

- looked at some teaching and learning aids in the application section

Chapter Seven

The mismatch between sounds and spellings in English and phoneme theory

What this chapter includes

7.1   The mismatch between sounds and spellings – an introduction

Few people would dispute the assertion that the spelling of British English is only a rough and ready guide to its pronunciation. If we need an example, consider the pronunciation of the vowel sound in the word 'hit' and then compare it with the underlined vowel sounds in the following words:

manage

receive

women

business

These are not unusual words, nor was it difficult to compile this list. The fact that all five written vowel characters are used somewhere in the language to represent the same sound must be fairly unnerving for foreign learners just as it can be a source of great difficulty for native children as they begin to familiarise themselves with the conventions of written English. We could, of course, find countless other examples of spelling anomalies in English.

George Bernard Shaw, one particularly well known figure in a long line of would-be spelling reformers, suggested tongue in cheek that the word 'fish' might as well be spelt 'ghoti'.

The 'logic' of his new spelling can be traced as follows:

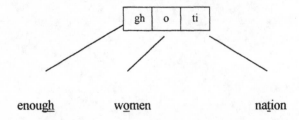

	gh	o	ti	

enough   women   nation

This joke, of course, ignores positional constraints (i.e. there is no English word that begins with 'gh' pronounced like the 'f' in fish – this pronunciation only occurs in word medial or final positions e.g. rough/rougher), nevertheless it does underline the serious point that the spelling of English is a terribly unreliable guide to the pronunciation of the language.

7.2   Some of the reasons for the mismatch

There are two different ways of looking at a language – these are usually dealt with under the headings diachronic and synchronic linguistics. A diachronic view of language considers the language as a historical phenomenon. The state of the language at any given time is accounted for by reviewing previous varieties of that language or its precursors. Thus a diachronic view of English would look at the way the language has developed and changed over the centuries and it would look at those earlier languages that had contributed to the formation of English.

A synchronic view of language, on the other hand, takes a cross-sectional slice of language at a given time and studies it without much or indeed any reference to earlier (or later) versions. Synchronic studies are nearly always concerned with the contemporary version of the language concerned.

In order to properly consider the gap between the pronunciation of English and its spelling we will have to take both a synchronic and a diachronic view of the language.

Synchronic studies are dominant in modern linguistics and we shall start by looking at the mismatch from a synchronic point of view. We all know that the English alphabet provides us with some 26 characters with which to represent the language visually. It would be reasonable to expect of an alphabetical writing system that symbols would have been created to reflect and represent the sounds of the language. English, however, has approximately 49 discrete speech sounds. (Approximately, because some accents have one or two more or fewer.) These distinct speech sounds are called phonemes and we will discuss them further and define them later in this chapter. Quite clearly, to have a reliable and consistent writing system which matched the speech system of English on a one-to-one basis we would need to have the same number of written symbols as we have phonemes and we would need to use them in a very deliberate way.

Here, then, we have the first reason why our written language is not a very good indicator of our pronunciation – there are simply not enough letters in our alphabet to go round. Here's an example to illustrate what we mean:

Bert

bout

boat

butt e.g. He's the butt of many cruel jokes.

but e.g. Naughty but nice.

bought

boot

bat

bet

bit

bait

bite

beat

All of these words are phonologically very simple. Their 'formula' is /b/ + vowel sound + /t/ and the only thing that distinguishes any one of them from the other twelve in speech is the vowel sound. But just look at the orthographic contortions that the language needs to signal this simple difference when it only has five vowel letters to play with!

If we now take a diachronic view of our language we will find still more reasons for the disparity between its written and spoken forms.

First, the alphabet itself does not 'belong' to English in any direct sense. It is basically the alphabet associated with Latin and even that was an adaptation of the alphabet of a different language altogether – Greek (hence the name, alphabet). It was imposed upon English in the 7th Century and not surprisingly it didn't (and doesn't) 'fit'.

Secondly, the written system has been, over the centuries, the subject (many might say the victim) of the attention of spelling reformers. Spelling reform is not, as many of us believe, a modern preoccupation and, in fact, some of the most bizarre mysteries of English spelling are simply the result of the tinkering of well-intentioned but sometimes poorly informed spelling reformers. Take for example a simple every day word like 'could'. Why is there a silent 'l' in it?

Some people point to 'would' and 'should' and say that 'could' clearly fits into some kind of pattern here. But 'would' and 'should' are related to 'will' and 'shall' respectively and so it is clear where the 'l's' come from. 'Could', on the other hand, has a similar relationship with 'can' not 'call' and we can only summarise that the 'l' is the gift of some long forgotten spelling reformer who get the wrong end of the stick and concerned him/herself with anything but the way the language was actually pronounced or the true relationships between particular words.

Thus we have two more reasons for the gulf between the written and spoken languages to add to our first – the alphabet was rather inappropriate in the first place and the written language has been distanced even more from the spoken languages by spelling reformers who gave greater priority to their own pet theories about, for example, word derivations than to the arguably pressing need to bring our orthography into line with our speech.

7.3   The intrinsic conservativeness of writing systems

There is one more important (and for our purposes, final) reason for the divergence
of the two forms of English. Written languages generally resist change whereas
spoken ones don't (or at least not to the same extent). At school we are all taught to
spell the language accordingly to norms that have been around for a long time. In
other words we are taught to spell English as our parents and grand-parents did and
we normally expect our children to fall into line when their time comes. It is
inconceivable, however, that we should be taught (in the vast majority of schools at
least) to speak in a particular way. If we are honest we don't even have a very clear
idea of how earlier generations did speak but a few seconds listening to Second
World War newsreels or even early television advertising features will quickly
demonstrate that pronunciation is almost as subject to change as fashions in
clothing.

If our writing systems were to keep up with our pronunciation they would probably
have to be revised every fifty years, say. They are not, and so to some extent writing
systems, if we know how to decode them, serve as a fossilised record of the
pronunciation of our forebears. It stands to reason, then, that the older a writing
system is the greater will be the gap between it and the current pronunciation of the
same language. As written systems go, English is getting on for being middle-aged
and thus for this reason too is unlikely to yield much helpful information to a learner
trying to decode the current state of pronunciation from it.

7.4   Why are we looking so hard at the written form of the
language in a book about phonetics and phonology?

One of our legitimate areas of interest as teachers of a language is the spoken form
of that language. In our case even more than most other language teachers we need
to free ourselves from the long established prejudices that painstaking (and often
painful!) study of writing convention leave us with.

We have to recognise that the written form of the language rather than the spoken
form is 'substandard'. It's a loaded word this but try to bear in mind that we are
using it almost technically. One of the prejudices about language that most of us
share is that the written language is its pure, ideal form and that speech is somehow

a corrupt and debased reflection of writing. From a linguist's point of view, the opposite is closer to the truth. Speech is the primary form of a language and the written conventions to which we all try to conform are a very poor and often apparently unsystematic secondary reflection of that primary form.

We need to give this matter considerable thought for two practical reasons. First, for our own sakes as providers of language models to our learners, we need to release ourselves from convictions about the way the language is 'supposed' to sound based on our preoccupation with spelling. Secondly we need to recognise that many of our learners are similarly predisposed to believe what they see written down rather than the evidence of their own ears. Thus, in the classroom, we will frequently find ourselves having to counter the effects of interference from the written form of the language in the pronunciation of our students.

7.5   Some attempts at classroom applications

Most of what we have said up to now in this chapter is designed to increase our awareness of the pitfalls of an over-reliance on the written form of English in a reasonable approach to its pronunciation.

Nevertheless some worthy TESOL practitioners have attempted to turn the minefield of spelling-sound relationships into a tool to help learners. In the scope of a book like this we can do no more than point out one or two of them out and leave the reader, if sufficiently intrigued, to follow the matter up for her/himself.

Foremost in recent years in insisting that the written form of English holds valuable phonological clues for learners has been Wayne B. Dickerson and in articles such as Orthography as a pronunciation resource (World Englishes Vol 6 No 1 pp 11-20, 1987) he puts forward some interesting arguments.

A whole methodology which, among other things, makes an early link between phonology and orthography is the 'Silent Way' devised and popularised by Caleb Gattegno (See Larsen-Freeman, (1986) for a short and clear description of the methodology). In this methodology early use is made of 'Fidel Charts'. These are arrangements in columns of all the conceivable spellings of particular sounds. In the case of English, of course, the resultant charts are fairly complex but at least they give learners the opportunity to link sounds with a wide range of potential orthographic realisations right from the beginnings of their exposure to English.

7.6   Phoneme theory – an introduction

7.6.1   Transcriptions

Though they have had very little real impact on the written language, there is no doubt that generations of would-be reformers of our spelling have had, collectively, a perfectly reasonable purpose.

The fact is, though, that they have not succeeded and this has meant that those who need to look at the language in a systematic way have been left with the task of finding an accurate way of representing speech visually. Such a representation is normally called a transcription. This book follows current practice in that it uses an appropriate subset of the transcription system devised and from time to time revised by the International Phonetics Association. (The initials of this Association are generally used to denote the full transcription system itself so don't be surprised to see IPA used in books about phonetics referring to a transcription system rather than an Association.)

Even within such a transcription system there are choices of application and depth of analysis to make. In general the major choice is between a phonetic transcription (often referred to as a **narrow** transcription) and a phonemic transcription (often referred to as a broad transcription). The difference is that a **phonetic** transcription attempts to account for all the many acoustic variations in the speech stream even when these are not 'significant' in the sense of distinguishing between two different words in the language or languages under study. **Phonetic** transcriptions, then, are valuable to those phoneticians and other linguists who are taking a very precise interest in very small details of speech sounds.

A **phonemic** transcription, in contrast, is concerned only with identifying and recording those sounds in a particular language or languages which actually make a difference to the meaning being communicated. As such it will not surprise the reader to learn that it is this form of transcription that will be used in the following chapters and which, in a very limited way, has been used in earlier chapters of this book.

A phonemic transcription, then, limits itself to having, and consistently using, a single symbol for each significant speech sound in the language, that is to say, for each <u>phoneme</u>. There is a complete list of the transcription symbols used in this book in Appendix A.

7.6.2   What is a phoneme?

Phonemes are the building bricks of any spoken language. They are the discrete sounds that we combine to make words. They are, in fact, the smallest segments of sound that can distinguish one word from another in a given language.

If, for example, we agreed that 'bet' and 'bat' are two different words it must be because whatever else they may have in common there must be at least one phoneme different between them. As we shall see in later chapters we would transcribe them as /bɛt/ and /bæt/ respectively. Be warned, incidentally, that we happen to have chosen an example of transcription here which on the face of it doesn't appear to be adding much in terms of accuracy to normal spelling. This is an illusion caused simply by the choice of words. Be reassured, for example, that in phonemic transcription the symbol /ɛ/ will always and only represent the sound of the 'e' in 'bet' whereas the letter 'e', of course, can represent a whole range of different vowel sounds or none at all in the many cases in English when it is a silent letter.

7.7   Complementary distribution and allophones

Say the following three words to yourself:

1   time

2   bat

3   little

Now try again, this time concentrating particularly on your production of the /t/ sound in each word. It should be fairly easy for you to notice that number three is radically different from numbers one and two. Your tongue should be very differently positioned as you say the /t/ sound in that word in comparison with the other two. Now go back to the first two – are they really the same? Try saying the two words with a lighted match in front of your mouth. Is there not a tendency for the /t/ of 'time' to blow it out whilst the /t/ of 'bat' doesn't seem to do so so readily?

What you are beginning to perceive is that there are variations of the /t/ phoneme in English (which would, of course, be recorded in a narrow phonetic transcription) which, unless you had previously studied phonetics, you, in common with every other native speaker of English, would have been blissfully unaware of. These are, in fact, variations which are not significant (in our technical sense of potentially distinguishing between two words in the language). Such variations are called allophones (in linguistics and other sciences the prefix allo- signals a non-significant variation, the suffix –eme signals a significant one).

These allophones of /t/ are allophones and not phonemes because in English they are in complementary distribution. In other words /t/ number three only occurs in certain predictable phonetic environments (i.e. in the middle of a word and in front of a particular set of consonant sounds). In English /t/'s numbers one and two never normally occur in the same environment.

Generally speaking native speakers of a language are conditioned during the initial language acquisition process to be quite insensitive to allophonic variation – we don't need to notice it and so we don't notice it – we've got quite enough to do without being aware of these variations which, in fact, add nothing to the message.

7.8   The language specificity of phoneme sets

We used the term 'conditioned' in the last paragraph to describe the way that during the process of native language acquisition each of us gets the capacity to divide up the range of speech sounds into approximately the same 49 units as every other native speaker of English. This division is by no means a universal feature of human language. Each language (and in a slightly different way each dialect of each language) divides up the available sounds uniquely. In this sense the divisions between one phoneme and another in a particular language are arbitrary. Although this is a very dangerous analogy, it may help to imagine the sounds available to English or any other language as a long line. English makes 49 divisions somewhere along that line. Some of the divisions are very close together, others are a long way apart and parts of the line are left untouched. Another language, though it uses the same line, may have its divisions in radically different spots. It may also use parts of the line that English ignores and, to add to the complications it is most unlikely to have 49 divisions. There may be more divisions or more probably substantially fewer. In comparison with most other languages English, with its 49 phonemes, is a bit on the rich side. You will find this particularly true of our vowel sound system.

The consequences of this in a language learning situation are fairly predictable. Imagine, for example, a Spanish speaker trying to decode spoken English. Her language is relatively limited in the number of vowel phonemes it has – there are five monopthongs – but she is listening to a language that meaningfully divides up virtually the same acoustic range with twelve vowel phonemes. Conditioned as she is to 'funnel' a variety of allophonic variations into five significant divisions, she continues to do so when listening to English. When the quality of a particular vowel sound is radically different from anything in her existing perceptual repertoire she may well hear it as a new sound but there will be many English phonemes that are close enough to Spanish allophones to be conflated.

7.9   Applications

Practitioners of ESOL differ considerably in the strategies that they adopt for dealing with the kind of ear-training whose necessity seems to be implied by the above. At one extreme there are those who advocate and practise total deliberate neglect. They prefer to spend their and their students' energy on suprasegmental phonology in the belief that sensitivity to the target segmental system will naturally be acquired so long as the learners' attention is on something else. At the other extreme are those who advocate substantial practice at the phoneme level as a preliminary to the production of larger units. In the middle are those who value the techniques of the latter group but reserve them for occasional remedial practice.

The authors of this book would probably find themselves alternating between the first and the last categories but this is not to be seen as a recommendation since teaching circumstances – so variable in TESOL – will ultimately have a considerable influence on the position a particular teacher takes on an issue like this.

7.9.1   The traditional use of minimal pairs

The teacher has diagnosed on some earlier occasion a particular pair of phonemes as being confused or at least needing a bit of attention. They are /ʌ/ as in 'suck' and /æ/ as in 'sack'. She prepares this part of a lesson by making a list of five minimal pairs – i.e. pairs of English words which are distinguished by the replacement of one phoneme for another (in this case, of course, by the vowel phoneme). Her list looks like this:-

1 /ʌ/	2 /æ/
suck	sack
cut	cat
bun	ban
lump	lamp
run	ran

(notice that the teacher is an R.P. speaker – there are many accents of English in which the first column would contain the vowel phoneme /ʊ/, and this is what a teacher with such an accent would teach).

In class she spends a few seconds explaining to the students that they are going to do some pronunciation practice for a few minutes before starting the lesson proper. Then she gives them a clear model of the first phoneme using the words from her list. She reassures the class that as they are focusing on pronunciation, it is not essential that they understand the words they are using. She has the class repeat her model chorally and individually until she is happy that everyone is making a reasonable approximation to the target vowel phoneme and she writes on the board:

1 /ʌ/
suck

Now she repeats the whole process with the second vowel phoneme. When that is complete her board looks like this:

1 /ʌ/   2 /æ/
suck   sack

The phonemic symbols are not pointed out to the class particularly but are simply there to add circumstantial evidence that there is a difference between the two sounds for learners having difficulty convincing themselves!

Now she randomly says the other words from her list and invites the class to instruct her as to which column she should write them in. The board finally looks like her original list.

Now she tells the class that she is going to say one of the words and they are not to repeat it but simply say if it is a 'number one' or a 'number two'. There then follows a drill which goes like this:

T.   suck

S1   one

T.   suck

S1   one

T.   ran

S1   two

T.   lump

S1	one
T.	lamp
S1	two
T.	bun
S2	one

etc, etc.

This is done fairly rapidly and on those occasions where a student gets an identification wrong the teacher immediately switches to another student so that the one having difficulty gets a chance to hear some more correct identifications before she comes back to him.

Towards the end of this procedure the teacher is getting pretty confident that the class can now perceive the difference between these two vowel sounds quite efficiently but she is well aware that we transmit information about vowel sound quality visually as well as acoustically. Lip-reading for hearing-impaired people would be very difficult otherwise. Visual clues such as lip-rounding, the degree of tension in cheek muscles and lower jaw position can be hidden from the students by the simple strategy of hiding the face with a sheet of paper, which she does from time to time as the students' confidence grows. This encourages the acquisition of aural discrimination skills that might otherwise not develop.

Now she asks the class to each take a piece of paper and a pencil and asks them to write down a list of letters, thus:

A:

B:

C:

D:

E:

She tells them that she is going to say five words, that she will repeat each word once, that they all come from the list on the board and that they are to do no more than write the **numbers** corresponding to the columns.

She reads out:

lump ..... lump

run ..... run

sack ..... sack

bun ..... bun

lamp ..... lamp

She then announces the result: 1, 1, 2, 1, 2.

She repeats this little test, using different selections of words, two more times and by now there is virtually 100% correct identification. At this stage she feels that she has achieved, for the moment at least, an acceptable level of recognition. So now she invites them all to make up their own lists, secretly, of five words and, in pairs, to administer to each other little tests as they have just been doing. After a few minutes she regroups them in fours and puts them through this process again, monitoring all the while to ensure that they are, individually, producing reasonable approximations to the target phonemes.

By this point a good ten minutes have passed since the beginning of the period and she calls a halt to the activity in order to begin the lesson proper. She knows that she has taken a small step towards improving her learners' recognition and production skills but she knows equally well that even for these two phonemes this is not the end of the story – she will need to review them and practise them further on later occasions.

7.10 Summary

In this chapter we have seen how for a variety of historic and other reasons the writing system of a language may not be a very reliable guide to its pronunciation. This has led us on to recognise that linguists need a more accurate visual representation of a language in order to be able to study it. We have gone on to see that applied linguists like language teachers need a transcription system that reflects the psychological realities of a language and not every possible acoustic detail. We have, therefore, settled on a <u>phonemic</u> transcription.

We have moved on to define the phoneme and noted in passing that phonemes are specific to the languages in which they occur. Finally we have looked at a simple application of phoneme theory in the classroom in the form of a short teaching procedure employing minimal pairs.

In other words we have:

- looked at the mismatch between the speech system and the orthography of English

- suggested a justification for having a systematic transcription system

- decided that a phonemic rather than a phonetic transcription is most relevant to language teachers

- looked at and defined phonemes

- considered the use of minimal pairs in pronunciation teaching

Chapter Eight

Phonemic transcription (part one)

What this chapter includes

8.1   Introduction

In the previous chapter we considered phoneme theory. In Chapter Eight we will be looking at particular features of phonemes as well as introducing the symbols used for transcribing the sounds of English. Many of these symbols will already be familiar as they are taken directly from the Roman alphabet. Others have been 'borrowed' from other alphabets or purposely invented. As was pointed out in the last chapter it is important not to get the 'normal' spelling of English confused with the phonemic system. Sometimes a phonemic symbol identical to a symbol of the alphabet may have a sound value rather different to that associated with it in ordinary written English.

Broadly speaking there are two groups of sound type, and we have been liberally referring to them already – consonant sounds and vowel sounds. Before we look at the phonemic symbols that represent them, let's consider their features in some more depth than we have so far allowed.

8.2   The consonant sound and the vowel sound

When we looked at the structure of the syllable we necessarily had to consider consonant sounds and vowel sounds. We mentioned, too, that the term consonant has two somewhat conflicting meanings – one used to refer to letters of the alphabet other than a, e, i, o and u, and one that refers to a particular kind of sound. It is the latter that we are interested in. In phonological terms, a consonant sound is a sound that involves the organs of speech (the tongue, the lips etc) taking up a position such that the normal flow of air outwards from the lungs is interfered with and noise is produced. There are various types of consonant sound and we shall be dealing in more detail with their articulation in Chapter Ten. The nature of the noise produced, though, can be in the form of an explosion of air (plosion) such as with consonant sounds like /p/, or friction – a hissing type sound – such as occurs with /f/ or /s/. Other consonant sounds are realised by having a blockage in the mouth and a flow of air through the nose (for example /n/ and /m/).

Vowel sounds on the other hand, do not have any direct obstruction in the mouth and are produced by a combination of lip and tongue positions. Vowel sounds also have syllabic significance and can, indeed, form syllables on their own in a few cases ('eye' for example is a single diphthong). Perhaps one reason for regional variation of pronunciation is the relative lack of specificity of the vowel sound as compared to the consonant sound. It is certainly the vowel sound which is most prone to change among speakers of English in the British Isles and beyond, when it comes to the pronunciation of particular words.

8.3 The phonemic symbols for English (R.P.)

Let's now take a look at the phonemic symbols used for transcribing the sounds of English. It's as well to point out again that the phonemes listed below are those found in Received Pronunciation English. In your own accent there may well be some slight differences in the rendition of one or two of the vowel sounds. This is not really important. As we said earlier R.P. is used in this book not for any qualitative reasons but for the sake of a widely recognised and accepted standard. When it comes to transcribing English the choice is yours as to whether you employ R.P. or transcribe directly from your own accent.

Note that phonemes are usually contained within slanted brackets.

8.3.1 Consonant sounds:

/b/ as in bed

/d/ as in door

/f/ as in fish

/g/ as in girl

/h/ as in hope

/k/ as in cat and kite

/l/ as in love

/m/ as in money

/n/ as in near

/p/ as in pen

/s/ as in sun

/t/ as in tie

/v/ as in view

/z/ as in zoo

All these symbols will be familiar to you, taken as they are directly from the alphabet. Note, though, that /k/ is used to represent the sound often associated with the letter 'c' – for example 'coat', 'candle', 'comfortable' all have initial /k/ in transcription. 'c' itself is not used in the phonemic transcription of English.

/r/ as in run

/w/ as in win

/j/ as in you

These three sounds are in many ways similar to vowel sounds – indeed, /w/ and /j/ are often referred to as semi-vowels – but as they cannot form the centre of a syllable they are classed as consonant sounds. Note here that the symbol /j/ does not have the same value in transcription as it does in spelling (see Chapter Twelve for further details).

/θ/ as in thin

/ð/ as in then

Here we have a case where a combination of letters that appear the same are pronounced differently. The spoken quality of the 'th' in 'thin' is at variance with the quality of the 'th' in 'then', and this is a distinction we will come to shortly.

/ʃ/ as in shoe

/ʒ/ as in measure, beige

/ŋ/ as in wing

Notice that in the last of the three symbols above, /ŋ/ the spelling combination 'ng' is rendered phonemically as a single sound. This phoneme also precedes velar consonant sounds – i.e. /k/ and /g/ - rather than /n/ as ordinary spelling would suggest. Hence 'sink' is /sɪŋk/ and 'anger' is /æŋgə/.

There are also two consonant sounds in English which are a combination of two phonemes. They are known as affricates. These are:

/tʃ/ as in <u>ch</u>in and pit<u>ch</u>

/dʒ/ as in gin and just

Although these involve a combination of sounds they are nevertheless classed as independent phonemes since they can form minimal pairs – e.g. 'tin' and 'chin' i.e. /t/ vs. /tʃ/.

8.3.2   Vowel sounds

As pointed out in Chapter Seven, normal orthography has problems when it comes to representing vowel sounds on paper, because there are only five vowel letters but, depending on accent, around twenty vowel sounds. Vowel sounds can be pure (monophthongs) or involve a glide from one vowel sound position to another (diphthongs) or have two glides subsequent to their initiation point (triphthongs). Here some care must be taken as there is little correspondence between the phoneme symbols for vowel sounds and the vowel letters of the alphabet.

The vowel sounds for R.P. are:

8.3.2.1   monophthongs

/i:/ as in t<u>ea</u> and s<u>ee</u>m

/ɪ/ as in t<u>i</u>n and p<u>i</u>t

/ɛ/ as in p<u>e</u>t

/æ/ as in c<u>a</u>t

/ɑ:/ as in c<u>ar</u>t

/ɒ/ as in p<u>o</u>t

/ɔ:/ as in p<u>our</u>

/ʊ/ as in g<u>oo</u>d and p<u>u</u>t

/u:/ as in f<u>oo</u>d and tr<u>ue</u>

/ʌ/ as in c<u>u</u>p and p<u>u</u>n

/ə/ as in <u>a</u>ttempt and moth<u>er</u>

/ɜ:/ as in b<u>ir</u>d and sl<u>ur</u>

8.3.2.2 diphthongs

/eɪ/ as in p<u>ay</u>

/aɪ/ as in h<u>igh</u>

/ɔɪ/ as in b<u>oy</u>

/aʊ/ as in n<u>ow</u>

/əʊ/ as in s<u>o</u> and <u>o</u>pen

/ɪə/ as in d<u>ear</u>

/ɛə/ as in c<u>are</u>

/ʊə/ as in c<u>ure</u>

8.3.2.3 triphthongs

/eɪə/ as in pl<u>ayer</u>

/aɪə/ as in h<u>ire</u>

/ɔɪə/ as in s<u>oya</u>

/aʊə/ as in c<u>ower</u>

/əʊə/ as in s<u>ower</u>

These symbols then will together allow us, at a phonemic level, to represent any English word. For example:

'trip' will be represented as /trɪp/

'beer' will be represented as /bɪə/

'hour' will be represented as /aʊə/

'clover' will be represented as /kləʊvə/

'child' will be represented as /tʃaɪld/

Note again that the diphthongs, triphthongs and the affricates count as just one phoneme. Hence, in the last of the examples above there are just four phonemes - /tʃ/ + /aɪ/ + /l/ + /d/ - even though there are six phonemic symbols.

Now let's try some fairly straightforward recognition exercises to start getting used to reading phonemic script.

8.4 Recognition exercises

Ex. 1

In the multiple choice items below what words are represented by the following phonemic transcriptions?

<u>example</u>

/pærət/   = part <u>parrot</u> port

/ɒpəreɪt/   = opera apparent <u>operate</u>

114

1 /dʒuːsɪ/ = jury juicy juice

2 /fræŋkfɜːtə/ = Frankenstein fretfully frankfurter

3 /kʌbəd/ = clubbed cupboard curbed

4 /ɪgzaːmpəl/ = example exemplary exemplar

5 /kɒnʃəns/ = conches concerns conscience

6 /lʌv/ = loaf love live

7 /kʌmpənɪ/ = company campaign camping

8 /dʒʊərɪ/ = during duly jury

9 /piːs/ = peace piece peas

Ex. 2

Now try identifying the correct phonemic transcription for the following words, again using a multiple choice format:

<u>examples</u>

fix	/fiːx/ /fɪx/ <u>/fɪks/</u>
old	/əʊld/ /ɔːld/ /ɒwld/
heed	<u>/hiːd/</u> /hɪəd/ /hɪd/

1 possibility = pɒssɪbɪlɪtɪ/ /pɒsɪbəl/ /pɒsɪbɪlɪtɪ/

2 coat = /cəʊt/ /kɒɑːt/ /kəʊt/

3 intervention = /ɪnvɛnʃən/ /ɪntəvɛnʃən/ /ɪntɛvʃən/

4 new = /njuː/ /njʊ/ /nʊ/

5 clear = /kəliːr/ /kliːr/ /klɪə/

115

6	president	=	/prezɪdənt/	/prezɪdənt/	/presdənt/
7	brother	=	/brʌðə/	/brʌðɛr/	/brʌthə/
8	woman	=	/wʊmaːn/	/wʌmən/	/wʊmən/
9	fourteen	=	/fɔːrtɪ/	/fɔːtiːn/	/fɔːtɪn/

8.5 Voice vs. voicelessness

Another important consideration when it comes to identifying phonemes is the nature of the vocal cords. These are found in the throat at the top of the **trachea** or windpipe. They have a biological function as well as being significant in the production of speech, being used to shut off the passageway to the lungs. They are, for instance, held tightly together when we lift heavy weights. They also, though, have the capability of vibration and can add voice to particular articulations. Let's take an example of this:

/s/ and /z/ are both sounds that involve friction. In their production the tongue is grooved down the middle and air is forced along this groove. When the air reaches the ridge behind the upper teeth (the **alveolar ridge**) it must pass through a narrow gap. As it does so, friction occurs. This much is true for both /s/ and /z/. So what then allows us to tell them apart? Since both /s/ and /z/ are durative type consonant sounds (i.e. they can be prolonged and produced for as long as a breath can last), we can get an idea of the contrast involved. Try producing a long /s/ and then, without stopping, change it into a /z/. What happens here is that for /s/ the vocal cords do not vibrate, they are held apart and the air from the lungs has a free passage until it reaches the point of friction. But in the case of /z/ the vocal cords are together and in order to escape the air must pass through them. As it does so the vocal cords vibrate. This vibration is called voice. Thus we can say that /s/ is a voiceless sound, whilst /z/ is voiced.

Many types of articulation (the way that a sound is produced by the various speech organs) fall into this voice vs. voiceless correspondence. Those consonant sounds that pair off in this way are:

/f/ voiceless	/v/ voiced
/p/ voiceless	/b/ voiced
/s/ voiceless	/z/ voiced
/t/ voiceless	/d/ voiced
/θ/ voiceless	/ð/ voiced
/ʃ/ voiceless	/ʒ/ voiced
/k/ voiceless	/g/ voiced

The only voiceless consonant sound in English that has no voiced equivalent is /h/, but there are a number of voiced consonant sounds that have no corresponding voiceless partner phoneme.

These are:

/l m n r w j ŋ /

All types of vowel sound: monophthong, diphthong and triphthong, are by their nature voiced (though see the section on /h/ in Chapter Ten).

Going back to /s/ and /z/ we can now consider their systematic occurrence as verb or plural inflexions.

As a third person singular marker for regular English verbs, /s/ follows voiceless phonemes (as in /wɜːks/, /lɑːfs/, sɪps/ etc) and /z/ follows voiced consonant sounds and vowel sounds. The exception to this rule is the sibilant consonant sounds – those that have a whistling/hissing sound: /s z ʃ tʃ dʒ / - as these all take the other available grammatical suffix /ɪz/. Hence 'oozes', 'forces', 'wishes', 'watches', 'hinges' will have the phonemic forms: /uːzɪz/, /fɔːsɪz/, /wɪʃɪz/, /wɒtʃɪz/, and /hɪndʒɪz/ (though some accents – for example Yorkshire – have /əz/ rather than /ɪz/).

The same pattern applies as far as plurals are concerned, with /s/ following voiceless consonant sounds (clocks etc) and /z/ following voiced consonant sounds and vowel sounds, whereas /ɪz/ follows sibilant consonant sounds.

Another pair of grammatically significant voiced and voiceless phonemes are /d/ and /t/ which along with /ɪd/ are employed to inflect the past tense form of the regular verbs in English. A similar type of pattern to the distribution of /s/, /z/ and /ɪz/ operates here. /t/ follows voiceless consonant sounds as in 'asked', 'wished' and 'coughed', whilst /d/ follows voiced consonant sounds and vowel sounds as in 'grabbed', 'waved' and 'paid'. /ɪd/ follows /d/ and /t/ themselves when they form part of the root of the verb as in 'needed', 'batted' etc, when, obviously a simple /t/ or /d/ inflexion would not suffice to mark the tense (though again, here, some accents have /əd/ instead.

A good test for detecting whether sounds are voiced or not is to plug your ears with your fingers as you pronounce them. If there is a buzzing noise this means the sound is voiced, lack of buzzing indicates a voiceless phoneme. You should be careful, though, with the voiceless sounds, that you produce just the consonant sound itself and not add a schwa /ə/, as this latter will have buzzing (since it is a vowel sound and as we said all vowel sounds have voice). Or, rather than isolating phonemes, you might try some together in actual words. Try, for instance, saying the world 'splendid' where the /sp/ segment is without voice and the rest of the word has buzzing (though /l/ is somewhat devoiced because of its proximity to /p/, but for our purposes at a phonemic level we need not worry about such phonetic conditioning).

Another test is to place a finger close to your Adam's apple and feel for vibration. The presence of vibration during production of a sound indicates voice, and lack of it is a sign of voicelessness. Try saying some more consonant sounds and then words using this technique.

8.6   Syllabic consonants

There are certain types of consonant sound (continuant in nature) that can, as it were, break the rules as regards syllabic structure. We saw earlier that a vowel sound forms the centre of a syllable and that consonant sounds have only marginal syllabic significance – i.e. they can only border the central vowel. However, there are in English five consonant sounds, that may, under certain circumstances, form syllables on their own. These are /l m n r/ and /ŋ/. Of these /r/, /ŋ/ and /m/ only

occasionally act in this manner. /l/ and /n/, on the other hand, often stand as
syllables in their own right.

For example, take the words:

    button   station   able   little

Many speakers would pronounce these using a syllabic consonant in final position.
Phonemically, then, these would be

    /bʌtn̩/   /steɪʃn̩/   /eɪbl̩/   /lɪtl̩/

In most cases, it is possible to also have a schwa plus a non-syllabic consonant
sound, i.e. /ə/ + /l/ or /ə/ + /n/ as in:

    /bʌtən/   /steɪʃən/   /eɪbəl/   /lɪtəl/

(though the last of these is somewhat unusual)

thus generating a structure that conforms to the rule we defined when we looked at
the nature of the syllable.

Whilst /n/, /m/, /r/, /l/ and /ŋ/ may form syllables for themselves and thus in this
respect are similar to vowel sounds, they are still classed as consonant sounds since
they share a number of significant features with other sounds considered
consonantal that may not have independent syllabic value.

Though it is skirting the issue somewhat, it is, perhaps, easiest to consider syllabic
consonant sounds as conditioned allophones of their mother phonemes. Since they
do not form minimal pairs (in the vast majority of cases) with their sister allophones
(of which there are a number in each case) they do not have phonemic significance.
Hence, for our purposes here, we will always cite them as /ə/ + /l/ etc with the
proviso that at a phonetic level no /ə/ may actually occur.

8.7 Applications

We saw in Chapter Seven a technique for drawing attention to and generating a pair of phonemes. Let's imagine that a teacher, either identifying needs amongst her class or trying systematically to expose her learners to a number of vowel phonemes, has done some minimal pair practice on a number of occasions. Sooner or later the need for some revision arises since, as we said when looking at minimal pair practice, once is seldom enough.

The teacher writes on the board ten words which differ only in their vowel sound:

peat

pet

part

port

pit

pat

pot

put

pert

pout

and briefly revises their pronunciation with the class. When she is satisfied that they have a reasonable grasp of the sounds involved i.e. they can both perceive and produce them with a fair degree of accuracy – she assigns a number to each word as follows:

peat 1

pet 2

part 3

port 4

pit 5

pat 6

pot 7

put 8

pert 9

pout 0

Then she explains that the class is going to compile a class telephone directory and she asks them to write on a piece of paper the names of their class mates (in large classes this can, of course, be done in subgroups). Then she starts the process off by dictating her own telephone number using the words on the board rather than the numbers themselves. Thus she says:

Pet, part, pat, pit, pert, pot, put

She checks quickly that the whole class has written down her telephone number as 2365978 and discovers that quite a few have put 2361978. Quickly she notes that further minimal pair practice is needed for the contrast between vowel sound 1 and vowel sound 5.

Each student then dictates their phone number (invented if they haven't got one, can't remember it or feel uncomfortable about making it public) and the teacher continues to gather further diagnostic information about the productive and perceptive skills of her learners.

8.8 Summary

In this chapter we have:

- considered definitions of vowel and consonant sounds

- looked at the role of voicing in the production of the phonemes of English

- presented the complete range of phonemic symbols necessary for reading phonemic transcriptions of English

- provided practice exercises in recognising such transcriptions

- considered the occurrence and role of syllabic consonants in English

8.9 Key to the exercises

Recognition exercise 1

1 /dʒuːsɪ/ = jury <u>juicy</u> juice

2 /fræŋkfɜːtə/ = Frankenstein fretfully <u>frankfurter</u>

3 /kʌbəd/ = clubbed <u>cupboard</u> curbed

4 /ɪgzaːmpəl/ = <u>example</u> exemplary exemplar

5 /kɒnʃəns/ = conches concerns <u>conscience</u>

6 /lʌv/ = loaf <u>love</u> live

7 /kʌmpənɪ/ = <u>company</u> campaign camping

8 /dʒʊərɪ/ = during duly <u>jury</u>

9 /piːs/ = <u>peace</u> <u>piece</u> peas

Recognition exercise 2

1 possibility = pɒssɪbɪlɪtɪ/ /pɒsɪbəl/ <u>/pɒsɪbɪlɪtɪ/</u>

2 coat = /cəʊt/ /kɒaːt/ <u>/kəʊt/</u>

3 intervention = /ɪnvɛnʃən/ <u>/ɪntəvɛnʃən/</u> /ɪntɛvʃən/

4 new = <u>/njuː/</u> /njʊ/ /nʊ/

5 clear = /kəliːr/ /kliːr/ <u>/klɪə/</u>

6 president = /prɛsɪdɛnt/ <u>/prɛzɪdənt/</u> /prɛsdənt/

7 brother = <u>/brʌðə/</u> /brʌðɛr/ /brʌthə/

8 woman = /wʊmaːn/ /wʌmən/ <u>/wʊmən/</u>

9 fourteen = /fɔːrtɪ/ <u>/fɔːtiːn/</u> /fɔːtɪn/

Chapter Nine

Articulation – part one: the vowel sounds

What this chapter includes:

9.1   Introduction

This is the first of two chapters on articulation – i.e. the actual physical production of speech sounds. For convenience we have dedicated this chapter to vowel sounds and the next to consonant sounds. In this chapter, then, we will look at the production of monophthongs (simple vowel sounds), diphthongs and finally triphthongs. We shall limit outselves to the consideration of only two articulators. (Articulators, in this sense means those parts of the anatomy which, whatever their primary biological purpose, are routinely used in the production of speech sounds by humans.) The articulators in question are the tongue and the lips.

9.2   Articulators involved in vowel production

9.2.1   The tongue

This is probably the most important articulator concerned with the production of vowel sounds. Since we do not tend to be too conscious of the position of the tongue during speech it often comes as a bit of a surprise to students new to articulatory phonetics to learn that its position in the mouth plays a crucial role in determining the quality of the vowel sound produced.

Before we look at its general position within the mouth let us briefly consider its parts. The tongue unfortunately does not have clearly identifiable segments – or at least any divisions it does have are not at points that are much use to linguists. In order to facilitate the description of the production of the speech sounds, therefore, linguists make some five divisions that may, in fact, look fairly arbitrary to an anatomist. The sections that interest us are: the tip, the blade, the front, the back and the root. They are illustrated on the following cross-sectional diagram of a head.

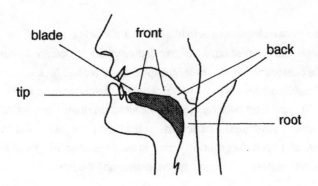

The labels are reasonably self-explanatory but beware the label 'front'. That is used a lot in the description of vowel production so please note that this is a relative term which contrasts with 'back' and that both the tip and the blade are further forward than the front.

It is the position of the tongue, then, as we said before, that more than anything else determines the quality of vowel sounds in English. There are two variables in terms of the tongue's positioning. First there is the question of the vertical distance between the tongue and the roof of the mouth, and secondly, since the tongue is a wonderfully flexible organ, there is the important question of which part of the tongue is raised highest.

Though, of course, there is almost infinite variation available on both axes, for practical descriptive purposes, linguists choose to distinguish between four vertical positions and three positions for the highest part of the tongue. The following diagrams illustrate some of these variations.

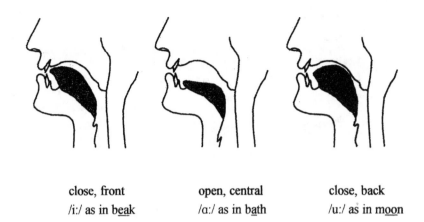

close, front	open, central	close, back
/iː/ as in b<u>ea</u>k	/ɑː/ as in b<u>a</u>th	/uː/ as in m<u>oo</u>n

9.2.2   The lips

The lips are not quite so central to the formation of vowel sounds in English as is the tongue but, nevertheless, they are for obvious reasons rather more visible than the tongue in normal circumstances. This means, of course, that they are more easily accessible to our (and our learners') conscious control. It is as well, therefore, to recognise that they are manipulated systematically when producing vowel sounds. The range of potential manipulation is again simplified for descriptive purposes into three positions – two extremes and one between the two extremes. They are:

(a) rounded (as in "oooo!")

(b) neutral   (as in "errrr…")

(c) spread   (as in "eeee!")

(a)

(b)

(c)

9.3 Cardinal vowels

Phoneticians normally talk about eight cardinal vowels. (These are sometimes referred to as primary cardinals but since we are not going to be concerned with the secondary ones we shall simply refer to them as the cardinal vowels.) These are not vowel sounds which necessarily occur in any natural language, but rather fixed points within the range available to the human articulatory system that are readily identified and thus can serve as reference points when describing vowel sounds that do occur in a given language.

The way of defining these cardinal vowels depends on one of the two articulatory variables that we have just been describing – tongue position. As we have seen this can be high, fairly high, fairly low and low and either the back, front or middle of the tongue may be the highest point.

Tongue positions and thus the resultant vowel sounds are normally represented on a chart like the one that follows and we have added to this the traditional labels used in phonetic descriptions – close/half or mid-close/half or mid-open/open.

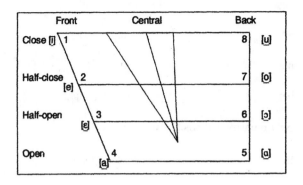

Ignoring the central areas, the eight intersections around the edge give us the eight cardinal vowels.

We can now, of course, superimpose on the same chart the twelve monophthongs or pure vowels of English. (Remember, we are talking here about R.P. – your own accent may differ slightly.)

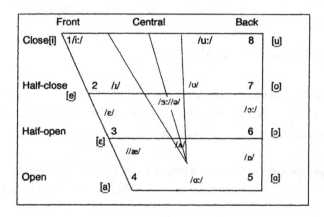

For the sake of convenience here is a list of English words, which in R.P. exemplify the vowel sounds:

/iː/	beat	/ʌ/	butt
/ɪ/	bit	/uː/	boot
/ɛ/	bet	/ʊ/	foot
/æ/	bat	/ɔː/	bought
/ə/	but (in unstressed positions)	/ɒ/	dog
/ɜː/	Bert	/ɑː/	guard

As you can see the existence of the eight cardinal vowel reference points allows us to make descriptive statements about the vowel sounds in R.P. or indeed any accent of any language such as:

/æ/ is about midway between cardinals three and four but slightly further back.

/uː/ is very close to cardinal eight but /ʊ/ is a little further forward and a little less close.

9.4 Classifying the vowel sounds

As you can see from the diagram, the vowel sounds of R.P. are not evenly spread around the chart. In fact they cluster into groups and we have two axes available to us to classify them.

For example, we can use the vertical axis and classify the vowel sounds as close, mid or open. If we do this there are four vowel sounds in each group, thus:

close: /iː/   /ɪ/   /ʊ/ and /uː/

mid: /ɛ/   /ə/   /ɜː/ and /ɔː/

open: /æ/   /ʌ/   /ɑː/ and /ɒ/

Alternatively, we can use the horizontal axis and classify them as front, central or back vowels. This time, why don't you try to classify them using the information presented in the vowel chart? You should be able to find four front vowels, three central vowels and five back vowels.

Ex. 1

> front:
>
> central:
>
> back:

9.5 Lip positions

In order to experience degrees of lip rounding, take a mirror and actually observe the position of your lips whilst saying the words in the following list or better still just the vowels. Draw a line when you think lip spreading stops and the lips have reached a neutral position, then draw a second line where you feel that the neutral position has been replaced by lip rounding.

Ex. 2

> /iː/ beat
>
> /ɪ/ bit
>
> /ɛ/ bet
>
> /æ/ bat
>
> /ə/ but (**un**stressed, remember!)
>
> /ɜː/ Bert
>
> /ʌ/ butt
>
> /ɑː/ guard
>
> /ɒ/ dog
>
> /ɔː/ bought

/ʊ/   foot

/u:/   boot

9.6 Diphthongs

Up to now we have been talking about monophthongs or pure vowels. In other words during the production of these vowel sounds, once the tongue and lips are in position to produce the vowel sound, they remain pretty well static for the whole duration of the vowel sound. The quality of the vowel sound is, thus, to all intents and purposes identical at the beginning and end of its production.

This does not have to be the case, however. English has a range of vowel sounds in which the tongue starts in one position and ends in another.

Take, for example, the vowel sound in the word 'fair'. It begins as /ɛ/ and ends as /ə/. The vowel sound here, then, is a diphthong – it is the smooth combination of two vowel sounds into one and during its production the tongue actually moves or the part of the tongue which is highest changes. In this case it is the latter, the change being from front to central.

In English we can distinguish two classes of diphthong. Firstly there are those like our example above where the highest part of the tongue changes. In these cases the movement is either from the front or the back of the tongue towards the centre and these are not surprisingly called centring diphthongs. Secondly there are those where the movement involved is from a relatively open to a relatively close position but using more or less the same part of the tongue – these are called closing diphthongs.

Here is a diagram of the initial positions of the eight diphthongs in R.P. The arrows indicate the direction of change and for clarity we have written example words below. In the exercise which follows try to classify the diphthongs as either centring or closing.

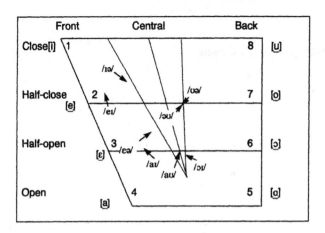

Example words

/ɪə/ fear

/eɪ/ hate

/ɛə/ fair

/aɪ/ height

/aʊ/ now

/əʊ/ boat

/ʊə/ poor (a fairly rare diphthong in English outside R.P. and some Scottish accents – you may not have it.)

/ɔɪ/ boy

Ex. 3

Centring	Closing
1.	1.
2.	2.
3.	3.
	4.
	5.

The correct answer to this question is, as usual, at the end of the chapter – when you have checked, you should notice that all the centring diphthongs finish in the schwa /ə/ position and all the closing diphthongs in either /ʊ/ or /ɪ/.

9.7 Triphthongs

As their name suggests, these vowel sounds (which are not terribly common) involve the tongue in three positions. There are only five of them in R.P. and all five end in schwa. They are, in fact, the five closing diphthongs with an additional final centring element, thus:

/eɪə/	player	/pleɪə/	
/aɪə/	liar	/laɪə/	
/aʊə/	our	/aʊə/	
/əʊə/	boa	/bəʊə/	NB Some people pronounce this as two syllables /bəʊwə/
/ɔɪə/	soya	/sɔɪə/	NB Some people pronounce this as two syllables /sɔɪjə/

9.8 Applications

There as long been intense debate within TESOL about the applicability of the kind of articulatory information outlined in this chapter within the ESOL classroom. Even those who are in favour of using it agree, however, that students respond much better to articulatory information about parts of the articulatory mechanism that they can consciously control. Thus degrees of lip-rounding are one area where students can be helped to fine-tune their vowel production. It must, however, be borne in mind that such procedures do, really, amount to little more than fine-tuning and that most students achieve reasonable vowel qualities in time with as little overt knowledge of tongue positions in English as they have in their native language!

9.9 Summary

In this chapter we have

- considered the two major articulators – the lips and the tongue

- considered lip rounding and spreading

- looked at the effect on vowel production of moving different parts of the tongue to different positions within the mouth

- looked at the reference points provided by the device of cardinal vowels

- seen that vowel sounds can be classified according to the features that they contain

- looked at the production of diphthongs and triphthongs

- briefly considered the limited applicability of this information to the classroom

- provided some practice exercises in classifying vowel sounds

9.10   Key to the exercises

Ex. 1

front:	/iː/, /ɪ/, /ɛ/, /æ/
central:	/ə/, /ɜː/, /ʌ/
back:	/uː/, /ʊ/, /ɔː/, /ɒ/, /ɑː/

Ex. 2

/iː/	beat	
/ɪ/	bit	
		spread
/ɛ/	bet	
/æ/	bat	

/ə/	but (**un**stressed, remember!)	
/ɜː/	Bert	
		neutral
/ʌ/	butt	
/ɑː/	guard	

/ɒ/	dog	
/ɔː/	bought	
		rounded
/ʊ/	foot	
/uː/	boot	

Ex. 3

Centring	Closing
1. /ɪə/	1. /eɪ/
2. /ɛə/	2. /əʊ/
3. /ʊə/	3. /aɪ/
	4. /aʊ/
	5. /ɔɪ/

Chapter Ten

Articulation – part two: the consonant sounds

What this chapter includes

10.1   The articulation of the English consonant sounds

In comparison with vowel sounds the consonant sounds are relatively easy to describe in terms of how they are produced. In most cases, there is some point of contact or near contact that may be felt. In this chapter, then, we shall be classifying all the consonant sounds of English with regard to their manner and place of articulation.

10.2   The articulation of the plosives

Plosives involve a direct blockage of the airstream from the lungs. The air builds up pressure behind the blockage, and then is released suddenly. English sounds articulated in this manner are /p b t d k g/

/p/, /b/

For /p/ and /b/ the blockage to the airstream occurs at the lips. There is a complete closure behind which pressure builds. Sounds made with a closure of the lips are known as bilabial. Thus /p/ and /b/ are bilabial plosives.

/p/ is a voiceless bilabial plosive, whilst

/b/ is a voiced bilabial plosive

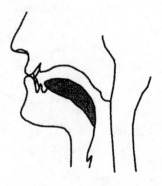

/t/, /d/

In the case of /t/ and /d/ the blockage occurs at the ridge behind the upper teeth. This is called the alveolar ridge and hence /t/ and /d/ have the label alveolar plosives.

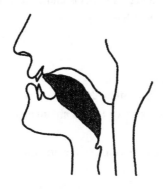

/t/ is a voiceless alveolar plosive

/d/ is a voiced alveolar plosive

/k/, /g/

Here the blockage is made between the back of the tongue and the soft palate or velum. They are known as velar plosives, /k/ being voiceless and /g/ voiced.

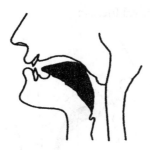

/k/ is a voiceless velar plosive

/g/ is a voiced velar plosive

10.3   The articulation of the fricatives

Fricative sounds involve some close narrowing but not total closure at some point of the oral tract (with one slightly anomalous exception as we shall see). In the case of such sounds, the air from the lungs is forced through the tight narrowing and a hissing or whooshing noise occurs. This is known as friction. There are eight regular fricatives in English. These are:

/ f v θ ð s z ʃ ʒ /

In addition to these eight /h/ is often also referred to as a fricative, though in this case a slightly more complex set of factors are involved than those outlined above.

Beginning then at the outermost point of the oral tract we have:

/f/, /v/

Both /f/ and /v/ are labio-dental fricatives – where 'labio-' refers to the lips and 'dental' to the teeth. For those two phonemes the upper teeth are in light contact with the lower lip and air is forced through them with friction. In the case of /f/ the vocal cords are held apart and thus there is no voice, whilst with /v/ the vocal cords vibrate.

Thus /f/ is a voiceless labio-dental fricative

/v/ is a voiced labio-dental fricative

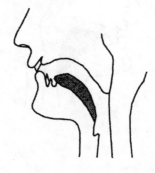

Moving slightly further back into the mouth as regards the place of articulation we have:

/θ/, /ð/

/θ/ and /ð/ are formed through contact of the tip and blade of the tongue with the upper teeth. For some speakers there may also be light contact between the blade of the tongue and the alveolar ridge, as well as the more primary dental contact. The form of contact produces a slit through which air is forced with friction. For this reason, /θ/ and /ð/ are referred to as slit fricatives. In the case of /θ/ there is no voice due to the vocal cords being held apart, thus allowing free passage of the air until the point of friction at the teeth. /ð/ on the other hand has vocal cord vibration and is thus voiced. Hence we label these phonemes:

/θ/ a voiceless dental slit fricative

/ð/ a voiced dental slit fricative

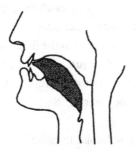

/s/, /z/

/s/ and /z/ are formed via contacts between the blade of the tongue and the alveolar ridge. Again there is light contact and air forces its way through and the tight narrowing with strong friction. Unlike /θ/ and /ð/, with this pair of phonemes the tongue is grooved down its medial line from front to back and it is along this channel that the air rushes. For this reason /s/ and /z/ are termed groove fricatives. The vocal cords are held apart for /s/ and vibrate for /z/. In this way:

/s/ is a voiceless alveolar groove fricative

/z/ is a voiced alveolar groove fricative

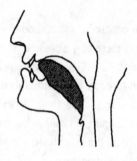

/ʃ/, /ʒ/

Similar in some ways to the articulation of /s/ and /z/ are the fricatives /ʃ/ and /ʒ/. The main point of difference is in the position of the body of the tongue. These phonemes are partly alveolar and partly palatal in that the body/front of the tongue is raised quite high towards the hard palate (that area of hard tissue immediately behind the alveolar ridge that stretches to the fleshy soft palate or velum). The point of contact of the tongue tip/blade is just a little further back than for /s/ and /z/, though again the air escapes via a medial channel. In the case of /ʃ/ the vocal cords are held apart whilst for /ʒ/ they vibrate. So:

/ʃ/ is a voiceless palato-alveolar fricative

/ʒ/ is a voiced palato-alveolar fricative

(Note the term palato-alveolar, like labio-dental, denotes that two places of articulation are involved in the production of the phoneme.)

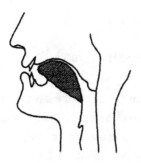

/ʒ/ is relatively rare in English, except in medial positions e.g. pleasure, measure (and even then its distribution is a good deal less than the other fricative phonemes).

We now come to the problem case:

/h/

/h/ seems to break the rules as we have so far described fricative realisation in that in some cases it does not involve a light contact or narrowing of the articulators. Take the word 'who' for example, which is conventionally transcribed phonemically as /huː/ or 'hot' which is transcribed /hɒt/ or 'hawk', transcribed /hɔːk/. In each of these cases there seems to be something approaching friction, but certainly not friction of the nature we have thus far considered. However, if we take the examples 'heat' /hiːt/, 'heed' /hiːd/ and 'heap' /hiːp/ there does seem to be more of a 'conventional' type of friction. The reason for this is that for /h/ the tongue always takes up the position of the following vowel sound during production and thus there are as many 'types' – or allophones – of /h/ as vowel sounds that may follow it. For /iː/ where the tongue position is quite close, there is sufficient narrowing for clearly perceptible friction to be detected. But for more open vowel sounds there is not, and what occurs instead is referred to as supraglottal friction – in other words the air 'whooshes' around in the oral cavity until the onset of voicing and the production of the vowel sound (which are, of course, simultaneous).

Some phoneticians, J. D. O'Connor for example, make a case for not considering /h/ as a separate phoneme at all, but looking on the sound that it (conventionally) represents as a strong voiceless version of the following vowel sound – and indeed there may be something in this. Again, though, for the sake of maintaining a norm at phonemic level, we shall transcribe words such as 'head', 'hard', 'hit', 'hat' etc with an initial /h/.

10.4   The articulation of the affricates

Affricate sounds are realised by a combination of the two types of articulation we have so far described. They begin with a stop and almost immediately have a fricative release. The only proviso for classifying an affricate as such is that the stop and fricative must share a common place of articulation. There are just two such phonemes in English. These are /tʃ/ and /dʒ/. Both are classed as palato-alveolar and both are realised by a primary point of contact slightly further back than is the case with /t/ and /d/. The initial phase involves the articulators taking up a position for a plosive, but this is not in fact sounded in the normal way (i.e. via an explosion of air). Note the difference here between a stop and a plosive proper – a stop refers to a total blockage of the airstream, whilst a plosive refers to the burst of air caused by a build- up of pressure behind the stop. What happens with an affricate is that there is near simultaneous release of the stop and the fricative element. The vocal cords are held apart for the voiceless /tʃ/ and vibrate for voiced /dʒ/. Hence we have:

/tʃ/ a voiceless palato-alveolar affricate

/dʒ/ a voiced palato-alveolar affricate

10.5   The articulation of the nasals

Nasal consonant sounds, as the name suggests, are formed partly by a flow of air through the nasal cavity rather than through the mouth. In order that this should happen, the soft palate has to be lowered and the air allowed to pass through the gap that is created. Compare, for instance, the difference between the alveolar plosives /t/ and /d/ and the alveolar nasal /n/:

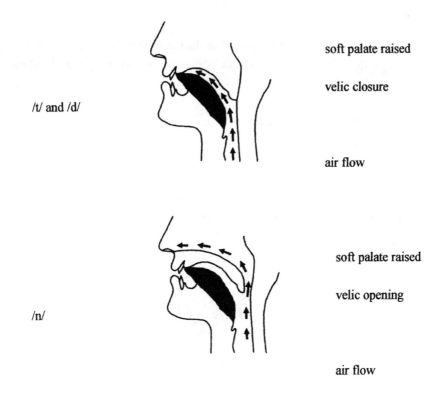

/t/ and /d/

soft palate raised

velic closure

air flow

/n/

soft palate raised

velic opening

air flow

There are three nasal sounds in English. These are /n m ŋ /. For all three the vocal cords vibrate.

/n/

/n/ is formed by a closure of the alveolar ridge and a free flow of air through the nasal cavity. To try to get an idea of the velum opening and closing and the soft palate rising and falling, make the stop for /d/ without releasing it and then pronounce an /n/. The lowering of the soft palate is what distinguishes these two articulations. Thus /n/ is classed as a voiced alveolar nasal.

For /m/ there is a blockage at the lips. Both the lips form a closure and hence this sound (like /p/ and /b/) is termed bilabial. Again the soft palate is lowered and air passes out through the nose.

/m/, then, is a voiced bilabial nasal.

/ŋ/

Here the closure is formed between the back of the tongue and the lowered soft palate/velum. Air passes directly into the nasal cavity.

/ŋ/

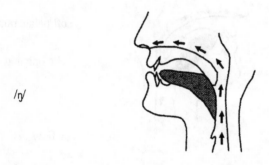

/ŋ/, then is a voiced velar nasal.

/ŋ/ frequently occurs in final position as the 'ng' in 'wing', 'thing', 'saying' etc and also before velar plosives as in 'sɪŋk/ and /ɪŋglɪʃ/. In English it cannot occur in initial position.

10.6   The articulation of the lateral /l/

There is only one lateral sound in English. This is the consonant sound /l/. The term lateral denotes that the release of air involved in the production of the phoneme is around the side of the tongue, whilst the tip approximates to the back of the upper teeth and the tongue blade makes a firm closure with the alveolar ridge.

/l/ is therefore termed an alveolar lateral. The vocal cords vibrate, giving voice.

There are two generally occurring types of /l/ that may be distinguished with some practice – even though we do not aurally detect the distinction in everyday conversation due to complementary distribution; these are dark /l/ and light /l/. The difference between these two allophones is that for dark /l/ the body of the tongue is raised towards the soft palate (i.e. it is velarised – a secondary form of articulation), whilst with light /l/ the body of the tongue is in a fairly low neutral position. Dark /l/ precedes consonant sounds (e.g. kiln, hilt, silk), /w/ (e.g. bulwark, stalwart) and comes at the end of words (e.g. wall, bill, sell). Light /l/ precedes vowel sounds (e.g. little – note here initial light /l/ and final dark /l/ - less, load) and /j/ (e.g. lure). If a word ending in /l/ is followed immediately by a vowel-initial word then light /l/ is likely to be used rather than dark /l/ (e.g. kill it).

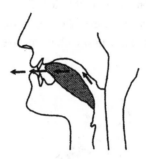

10.7   The articulation of the frictionless continuants

To complete our inventory of the articulation of the English consonant phonemes we turn to three sounds which are, perhaps, slightly marginal in classification as such. In many ways the three frictionless continuants of English /r/, /w/ and /j/ are similar to vowel sounds in that there is no direct obstruction in the vocal tract and it is the tongue and lip positions that play an important part in their realisation. This is particularly true of /w/ and /j/.

/w/

/w/ is a voiced labio-velar frictionless continuant. That is to say that the lips and the velum are paramount in its production. /w/ usually has fairly close lip rounding and the back of the tongue raised towards the soft palate. In this way it is similar to the vowel sound /u:/. The difference between /w/ and the close back vowel is that the tongue is slightly further forward. To get an idea of this try saying the word 'woo' until you get an idea of the glide for /w/ to the vowel sound /u:/.

Lip position for /w/

/j/

With /j/ the front of the tongue is raised high towards the high palate – but not close enough to create friction. This phoneme, then, is described as a palatal frictionless continuant. It is similar in some ways to the close front vowel /i/ but again involves a glide from initial position to that of the following vowel sound. Thus, with the archaic 'ye' /ji:/ the glide is slight, whilst with words like 'yes', 'you' and 'yonder' the glide is more pronounced.

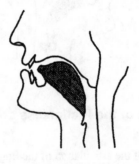

/r/

/r/ is also termed a frictionless continuant and again is most often realised as a glide from the original articulatory position to that of the following vowel sound. In initial realisation the tongue tip is somewhat behind the alveolar ridge and curls upwards slightly. Unlike /j/ and /w/, /r/ does not have a close vocoid counterpart and is not normally classed as a semi-vowel as the two former phonemes are.

/r/ is labelled a voiced post-alveolar frictionless continuant.

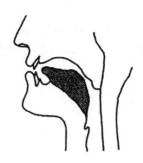

Finally, it should be noted that, although /r/, /w/, and /j/ share certain qualities with the vowel they are properly termed consonant sounds (in English R.P. at least) since they cannot form the centre of a syllable of the structure CVC. They may have only marginal syllabic value, i.e. they occupy only the C – or consonant – position. Moreover, they may occupy (again in R.P.) only the initial position in a syllable thus underlining their lack of versatility vis-à-vis the vowel.

We can summarise the articulation of consonant sounds in tabular form for the sake of convenience and easy reference. In the table below, we begin at the outermost place of articulation and work inwards. Manner of articulation is indicated along the vertical axis, place of articulation along the horizontal axis.

	bilabial	labio-dental	dental	alveolar	post-alveolar	palato-alveolar	Palatal	velar	glottal
plosive	p b			t d				k g	
fricative		f v	θ ð	s z		ʃ ʒ			h
affricate						tʃ dʒ			
nasal	m			n				ŋ	
lateral				l					
frictionless continuant	w				r		j		

Notes

- In cases where there are pairs of phonemes – i.e. those that share a common place of articulation – the phoneme to the left is voiceless and its counterpart to the right is voiced.

- For the sake of convenience, /w/ is classed here as a bilabial frictionless continuant, though it is properly labio-velar.

10.8 Fortis and lenis consonant sounds

Though we have spoken so far about voiced vs. voiceless consonant sounds, a rather more precise means of classifying them is in terms of their force of production – that is with how much energy they are realised. Roughly, we can say that what we routinely call voiceless consonants are realised with rather more energy and, in some cases, aspiration (audible escape of air) than voiced consonant sounds. This is because voiceless consonant sounds, by their nature, do not have the extra barrier – along with the direct point of articulatory obstruction – of the vocal cords. Hence, by the time the exhaled air reaches the point of obstruction, it still has a good deal of force left. Voiced consonant sounds must, of course, be produced by air from the lungs that has had to pass through the vocal cords and this necessarily 'weakens' their articulatory force. This distinction is known as fortis/lenis. Fortis consonant sounds are strong articulations (such as /p t k/) whilst lenis consonant sounds are weak (such as /b d g/). This distinction has an effect upon vowel sounds that precede consonant sounds. For example, contrast the minimal pairs 'at' and 'add', 'hop' and 'hob', 'clock' and 'clog' – in each case the vowel sound that precedes fortis consonant sounds is perceptibly shorter than the same vowel sound when it precedes lenis consonant sounds. Again, though we are not consciously aware of it, this effect of a following consonant sound on a vowel sound is crucial in effective decoding of spoken English.

10.9 Applications

Following on from the above section regarding fortis and lenis consonant sounds, one rather slight by useful technique for learners from speech communities that do not have the same distribution of voiced vs. voiceless consonant phonemes is to demonstrate the aspiration (and lack of it) with particular minimal pairs.

Arabic learners of English, for example, tend to have problems in distinguishing /p/ and /b/ since no independent /p/ phoneme exists in Arabic. The difference, therefore, that we take for granted, is not at all obvious to learners from Arabic-speaking countries, and such learners find the production of /p/ quite problematic.

As we have just seen, one of the differences between /p/ and /b/ is that /b/ has voice whilst /p/ does not, so one thing that we could do to try to get Arab learners to master /p/ is to get them to whisper /b/. This gets rid of the voice but there is another factor that more precisely distinguishes /p/ from /b/ for English speakers. Again we've just considered it. /p/ is a fortis consonant sound and /b/ is a lenis one. There is au audible puff of air that follows the release of /p/ that is not a feature of the articulation of /b/. This aspiration may be visually demonstrated by simply holding a strip of paper in front of your mouth and then articulating and releasing first a /b/ and then a /p/. The /b/ will hardly move the paper, but the /p/ will move it quite considerably. If you use tissue paper the effect will be even more striking. This can be easily demonstrated to a class and some minimal pair practice can be given to help consolidate the point. Learners can be asked to say, for example, first 'pan' and then 'ban'. There are many pairs of words in English that are distinguished solely by having /b/ or /p/ in initial position. A candle or a lighter will do the same job. Place the candle or flame about twelve to fourteen inches from your mouth and say a pair of words that begin with /b/ and /p/. **You do need to be careful** though, that the pairs you select don't have another aspirated sound in them somewhere as this will confuse the issue. The /b/ word will have little or no effect on the flame but the /p/ will move it significantly in the case of the candle and extinguish it completely in the case of the lighter. Again you can get the class to try it out for themselves, the idea being to blow out the flame and thus have produced a /p/ (NB the "lighter" option will also give you information as to who in the class smokes and depending on your own bent, you could start up a little debate about smoking or simply identify individuals who you can borrow cigarettes from during the break when you've run out!).

10.10 Summary

In this chapter we have:

- considered the articulation of the English consonant sounds in the following order:

  - plosives
  - fricatives
  - affricates
  - nasals
  - the lateral /l/
  - frictionless continuants

- looked at the distinction between fortis and lenis consonant sounds

- described a number of simple devices for drawing students' attention to the fortis/lenis, voiced/unvoiced, aspirated/non-aspirated distinction

Chapter Eleven

Phonemic transcription (part two)

What this chapter includes

11.1 introduction

11.2 symbols used in this chapter

11.3 a special note on some vowel symbols in phonemic transcription

11.4 transcription exercises 1-8

11.5 applications

11.6 summary

11.7 key to the exercises

11.1 Introduction

In this chapter we are going to begin practising productively the transcription skills that were introduced from a recognition point of view in Chapter Eight. Since gaining a productive skill involves a bit more work than gaining a recognition skill, we have spread it over two chapters instead of one. In this chapter we will concentrate on transcribing words, and later sentences which contain the monophthongs (i.e. the simple vowels) and those consonant sounds which are straightforward in phonemic transcription because the transcription uses the same symbol as our normal writing system.

There are three things to bear in mind when doing the transcription exercises in this book. First, for the sake of having a standard, remember, we are using R.P. as the transcription norm. If your own accent is not R.P. there will be a number of key phonemes (normally vowel phonemes) where, if you use your own accent, you will have a different transcription from that in the key. Remember neither of us is right and neither of us is wrong – we simply have different accents. To avoid this you can, of course, imagine an R.P. speaker and transcribe his/her accent, rather than your own – it's up to you.

The second point is of rather more general importance. After everything we said in Chapter Eight about the unreliability of our spelling system when it comes to foreign learners predicting pronunciation, it must be obvious that we are at risk of falling into similar traps when using the written system as a stimulus for transcription. You are going to have to be continually on your guard to avoid being misled by the spelling system. Each time you look at a word on the page, say it to yourself – if possible aloud – make sure you then don't transcribe any silent letters and that you resist the inclination we all have to see transcription as a way of encrypting written language. Keep reminding yourself that it is the **spoken** language you are trying to represent systematically.

Silent letters are a particular problem in English. The fall broadly into two categories – first the letters that are totally and obviously redundant, e.g. the 'b' in lamb. However essential that 'b' may be in our written conventions it is simply not there phonologically speaking and so our transcription will be /læm/.

More insidious are those silent letters which are adjacent to and influential on another phoneme.

Take, for example, the pair of words

'bid'   'bird'

The first one transcribes easily - /bɪd/ but the second is at first sight problematic. That 'r' is doing something, isn't it? It's signalling a special value of the preceding 'i' but it is nevertheless not being pronounced in its own right. (Not in R.P. at least.) Thus the transcription in this case will be:

/bɜːd/ **not** /bɜːrd/

The third point to keep reminding yourself of during transcription exercises is that features like punctuation and capital letters, vital though they may be in the written form of our language have no place in these exercises. The lengths of pauses indicated by full stops, commas etc and the suprasegmental features indicated by exclamation marks and question marks have a place in some forms of transcription and we have talked about them in earlier chapters but capital letters are a purely visual convention – so resist the temptation to capitalise phonemic symbols – it can't be done!

11.2   Symbols used in this chapter

First, as we said earlier, we are going to use all the monophthong symbols in this chapter. Just to remind you, here they are with examples using simple words containing the vowel phoneme concerned in R.P.

/iː/	bead
/ɪ/	bid
/ɛ/	bed
/æ/	bad
/ʌ/	bud

/ʊ/	good
/ɑː/	bard
/ɒ/	God
/ɔː/	board
/uː/	booed
/ə/	aft<u>er</u>
/ɜː/	bird

And then we are going to use all the straightforward consonant phonemes –

i.e.:

/b/   /d/   /f/   /g/   /h/   /k/   /l/

/m/   /n/   /p/   /r/   /s/   /t/   /v/

/w/   /z/

Before we start trying some actual transcription exercises let's briefly look at the letters of the alphabet which have been left out and why.

Amongst the vowel sound symbols the letters 'e' and 'o' are missing because they represent in the I.P.A. transcription system vowel sounds which do not actually occur in most varieties of English (as pure vowels at least – though we'll see /e/ later in a diphthong).

Amongst the consonant symbols the following are missing:

'c' – In writing this letter routinely represents one of two very different sounds in English – i.e. as in 'cat' and 'face'. In the former case it is transcribed as /k/ and in the latter as /s/.

'j' – This letter has not been used. It will not be used in this chapter for reasons made clear below under 'y'. Please note that when it is used in phonemic transcription of English it can sometimes appear without a dot.

'q' – This letter is not used in phonemic transcription. A word like 'queen' will be transcribed /kwiːn/ and a word like lacquer will be transcribed as /lækə/.

'x' – This letter is not used in phonemic transcription of R.P. When it is used as a phonemic symbol it represents the final consonant sound in the Scottish word 'loch'.

'y' – This letter is not used as a transcription symbol in R.P. when it occurs in words like 'yacht' it is transcribed as we shall see in the next chapter with the symbol /j/ thus /jɒt/.

11.3   A special note on some vowel symbols in phonemic transcription

People are sometimes confused by what seems to be a mismatch between the symbols that we employ in this book and the vowel sounds that they estimate themselves to be producing. A case in point here is the distinction that we make between /iː/ and /ɪ/. This seems to apply particularly with words such as **city** and **lovely**, where people often feel that they pronounce the final sound as /iː/ rather than /ɪ/. One reason for this is that people often examine these words in isolation rather than in connected speech. Isolating the word sometimes has a detrimental effect on arriving at a fair analysis of its component sounds, and this is particularly the case with sounds that come at the end of a word.

We have to reach some form of compromise between symbols and the minute, but noticeable, differences that occur in any individual's pronunciation as regards vowels in various phonetic environments.

To go back to the /iː/ vs /ɪ/ debate, we can see this compromise in action. The sound that the vast majority of speakers produce here in word-final position in connected speech is in fact somewhere between /iː/ and /ɪ/. However, it is nearer (in tests which have been done on this very thing) to /ɪ/ than it is to /iː/. So since we are applying qualitative measurement here we show it as /ɪ/. This compromise has the force of a transcription convention so that words like 'pretty' and 'city' are transcribed with a final /ɪ/ even when they are themselves at the end of a sentence, where **phonetically** they would be closer to /iː/.

This same type of compromise explains a range of symbol–sound representations. This is certainly true of the diphthongs. There are several diphthongs in English whose component parts are not exactly the same as any of the pure vowel phonemes. So please note their exact formation when you are transcribing.

This is not a random selection of symbols but the nearest we feel we can get to adequately representing the sounds of the language. No doubt you will come across other systems – there are a number that are current. Systems from, say, the US will be quite different from those of British English since the compromises they are making and the qualitative representations they are making vary.

11.4 Transcription exercises

 Transcription Exercise One

Transcribe the following words:

1	bed _____	2	wheeze _____
3	fig _____	4	vat _____
5	hark _____	6	rut _____
7	cool _____	8	loom _____
9	board _____	10	what _____
11	curl _____	12	batter _____

Transcription exercises two and three are set out below for those readers who feel they need extra practice of this kind of transcription.

Transcription Exercise Two

Transcribe the following words

1   pull _____   2   dart _____

3   love _____   4   woof _____

5   halve _____   6   moos _____

7   lop _____   8   lip _____

9   live (verb) _____   10   Paul _____

11   debt _____   12   laugh _____

Transcription Exercise Three

Transcribe the following words

N.B. This exercise draws attention particularly to silent letters.

1   naff _____   2   keys _____

3   rough _____   4   cars _____

5   dirt _____   6   because _____

7   whiff _____   8   vase _____

9   Mars _____   10   ward _____

11   enough _____   12   wood _____

Transcription Exercise Four

This exercise contains slightly longer words.

1   target _____   2   lager _____

3   photographer _____   4   Madonna _____

5   bullet _____   6   kilometre _____

7   distance _____   8   dollar _____

9   garden _____   10 calibre _____

11 distraught _____   12 lipstick _____

Transcription exercises five and six provide extra practice in transcribing longer words for those who feel they need it.

Transcription Exercise Five

1   pencil _____   2   zebra _____

3   removal _____   4   police _____

5   supported _____   6   splinter _____

7   replete _____   8   cleaner _____

9   daughter _____   10 pistol _____

11 whispered _____   12 flatter _____

1   perusal _____

2   terrible _____

3   luminous _____

4   comfortable _____

5   forgotten _____

6   dustbin _____

7   staffroom _____

8   university _____

9   palace _____

10   revolted _____

11   grovelled _____

12   particle _____

Now we will go on to transcribing short sentences. At this stage it will be convenient to 'pretend' that the sentences are made up of separate words. In the next chapter we will look at the more important 'boundary effects' of adjacent words in the speech stream.

  Transcription Exercise Seven

1   We were confident he'd come.

_____

2   Pat sends her best regards.

_____

3   His girlfriend looks lovely.

_____

4   He's got all a man could want.

_____

5   It's an odd number.

_____

6   Give me six apples, please.

_____

7   Consider what he's done!

_____

8   What's her address?

_____

9   Can he speak in a western accent?

_____

10   Have a good trip!

_____

11 See what Lucy can do.

_____

12 If he looks under seat number two he will see a parcel.

_____

Once again, the transcription exercise that follows, number eight, is provided for those people who feel they need extra practice.

◁》 **Transcription Exercise Eight**

1 Have a heart, mister!

_____

2 We've never seen her before.

_____

3 On Monday he spent twenty pence.

_____

4 His victims were teased mercilessly.

_____

5   He had several good breakfasts.

_____

6   All of us agreed happily.

_____

7   Peta went to Number One clinic.

_____

8   When Ted comes, give him some dinner, please.

_____

9   Meet me in a restaurant.

_____

10   It's a silly business, isn't it?

_____

11   Alex has an enormous bruise on her knee.

_____

11.5   Applications

It may seem strange even to consider practical classroom applications from such a teacher-centred skill as the ability to transcribe one's own language phonemically.

Nevertheless many colleagues insist that once they had themselves gained reasonable confidence in producing transcriptions accurately, they felt they were in a position gradually and incidentally to introduce the symbols to their classes.

Such teachers stress that they do not do so in any systematic way but only pull this particular rabbit out of the hat when it helps them to illustrate some phonological point.

Examples of this are providing headings for groups of minimal pairs or illustrating on the board that from a pronunciation point of view there really is nothing between the 'f' and the 't' of comfortable.

Small return, one might say, for the substantial investment required to acquire this skill.

"No", they answer, "You miss the point". Such graphic illustrations of otherwise elusive phonological points save so much time that a case could be made for them justifying the effort involved in learning to do it but they are essentially ephemeral. By their occasional use, however, a long-term recognition skill is being given to the students. Little by little without it ever appearing to be an intolerable extra burden, the students are being given the ability to decode phonemic transcription. The real pay-off comes with dictionary use. Over and above the other valuable benefits that a dictionary can provide to its user, good learners' dictionaries also normally give a phonemic transcription of each entry. To a learner who has never been exposed to phonemic transcriptions the mysterious symbols will obscure rather than clarify the pronunciation of the word in question. But a student equipped with a recognition knowledge of these symbols has a key to this valuable information which can be used on countless occasions.

11.6 Summary

In this chapter we have

- looked at one or two of the traps that people fall into when doing phonemic transcriptions

- introduced the symbols for the monophthongs in English

- introduced the consonant sound symbols where these coincide with letters of the alphabet

- noted those letters of the alphabet which are not, or rarely, used as transcription symbols

- considered ways of actually writing some of the more unusual symbols

- provided some practice in the combination of the symbols introduced so far in transcription at word and sentence level

- considered the application of transcription skills in the classroom for the development of recognition skills among our students that can be transferred to their own dictionary use

11.7 Key to the exercises in this chapter

Transcription Exercise One

1	bed ... /bɛd/...	2	wheeze ... /wiːz/...
3	fig ... /fɪg/ ...	4	vat ... /væt/...
5	hark ... /hɑːk/...	6	rut ... /rʌt/...
7	cool ... /kuːl/...	8	loom ... /luːm/...
9	board ... /bɔːd/...	10	what ... /wɒt/...
11	curl ... /kɜːl/...	12	batter ... /bætə/ ...

Transcription Exercise Two

1	pull ... /pʊl/...	2	dart ... /dɑːt/...
3	love .../lʌv/...	4	woof .../wʊf/...
5	halve .../hɑːv/...	6	moos .../muːz/...
7	lop .../lɒp/...	8	lip .../lɪp/...
9	live (verb) ... /lɪv/...	10	Paul .../pɔːl/...
11	debt .../dɛt/...	12	laugh .../lɑːf/...

Transcription Exercise Three

1	naff .../næf/...	2	keys .../kiːz/...
3	rough .../rʌf/...	4	cars .../kɑːz/...
5	dirt .../dɜːt/...	6	because .../bɪkʌz/...
7	whiff .../wɪf/...	8	vase .../vɑːz/...

9 Mars .../mɑːz/

10 ward .../wɔːd/...

11 enough .../ɪnʌf/...

12 wood .../wʊd/...

Transcription Exercise Four

1 target .../tɑːgɪt/...

2 lager .../lɑːgə/...

3 photographer .../fətɒgrəfə/...

4 Madonna .../mədɒnə/...

5 bullet .../bʊlɪt/...

6 kilometre .../kɪlɒmɪtə/...

7 distance .../dɪstəns/...

8 dollar .../dɒlə/...

9 garden .../gɑːdən/...

10 calibre .../kælɪbə/...

11 distraught /dɪstrɔːt/

12 lipstick .../lɪpstɪk/...

Transcription Exercise Five

1 pencil .../pensɪl/...

2 zebra .../zɛbrə/ or /ziːbrə/

3 removal .../rɪmuːvəl/...

4 police .../pəliːs/

5 supported .../səpɔːtɪd/...

6 splinter .../splɪntə/

7 replete .../rɪpliːt/...

8 cleaner .../kliːnə/...

9 daughter .../dɔːtə/...

10 pistol .../pɪstəl/...

11 whispered .../wɪspəd/...

12 flatter .../flætə/...

Transcription Exercise Six

1 perusal .../pəruːzəl/...

2 terrible .../tɛrɪbəl/...

3 luminous .../luːmɪnəs/...

4 comfortable .../kʌmftəbəl/...

5 forgotten .../fəgɒtən/...

6 dustbin .../dʌsbɪn/...

7   staffroom .../stɑ:fru:m/ or   8   university .../ju:nɪvɜ:sɪtɪ/...

/stɑ:frʊm/...

9   palace .../pælɪs/...   10 revolted .../rɪvəʊltɪd/...

11 grovelled .../grɒvəld/...   12 particle .../pɑ:tɪkəl/...

Transcription Exercise Seven

1   We were confident he'd come.

    .../wɪ wə kɒnfɪdənt hɪd kʌm/...

2   Pat sends her best regards.

    .../pæt sendz hɜ: best rɪgɑ:dz/...

3   His girlfriend looks lovely.

    .../hɪz gɜ:lfrend lʊks lʌvlɪ/...

4   He's got all a man could want.

    .../hɪz gɒt ɔ:l ə mæn kʊd wɒnt/...

5   It's an odd number.

    .../ɪts ən ɒd nʌmbə/...

6   Give me six apples, please.

    .../gɪv mɪ sɪks æpəlz pli:z/...

7   Consider what he's done!

   .../kənsɪdə wɒt hɪz dʌn/...

8   What's her address?

   .../wɒts hɜː ədrɛs/..

9   Can he speak in a western accent?

   .../kən hɪ spiːk ɪn ə westən æksənt/...

10 Have a good trip!

   .../hæv ə gʊd trɪp/...

11 See what Lucy can do.

   .../siː wɒt luːsɪ kən duː/...

12 If he looks under seat number two he will see a parcel.

   .../ɪf hɪ lʊks ʌndə siːt nʌmbə tuː hɪ wɪl siː ə pɑːsəl/...........................

Transcription Exercise Eight

1   Have a heart, mister!

   .../hæv ə hɑːt mɪstə/...

2   We've never seen her before.

.../wɪv nevə siːn hɜː bɪfɔː/...

3   On Monday he spent twenty pence.

.../ɒn mʌndɪ hɪ spent twentɪ pens/...

4   His victims were teased mercilessly.

.../hɪz vɪktɪmz wə tiːzd mɜːsɪləslɪ/..

5   He had several good breakfasts.

.../hɪ hæd sevərəl* gʊd brekfəsts/... *or .../sevrəl/................................

6   All of us agreed happily.

.../ɔːl əv əs agriːd hæpɪlɪ/..

7   Peta went to Number One clinic.

.../piːtə went tə nʌmbə wʌn klɪnɪk/..

8   When Ted comes, give him some dinner, please.

.../wen ted kʌmz gɪv hɪm səm dɪnə pliːz/...

9   Meet me in a restaurant....

.../miːt mɪ ɪn ə restəront/...

10 It's a silly business, isn't it?

...√ıts ə sılı bıznıs ızənt ıt/...

11 Alex has an enormous bruise on her knee.

...√ælıks hæz ən mɔːməs bruːz ɒn hɜ niː/...

12 God bless us!

...√gɒd blɛs əs/..

Chapter Twelve

Phonemic transcription (part three)

What this chapter includes:

12.1 introduction

12.2 all phonemic symbols not covered in Chapter 11

12.3 transcription exercises 9-12 using the full phonemic transcription system

12.4 assimilation

12.5 elision

12.6 linkage

12.7 transcription exercise 13

12.8 applications

12.9 summary

12.10 key to the exercises

12.1 Introduction

In Chapter Eleven we looked at the 'straightforward' consonant symbols used in transcribing English along with the twelve monophthongs of R.P. In this last chapter on phonemic transcription, we shall deal with the consonant sounds that are represented by symbols other than those taken from the Roman alphabet and also the symbols for the diphthongs and triphthongs of R.P. We will then be in a position to transcribe any word found in the R.P. accent of English. However, as was mentioned in the last chapter, when it comes to transcribing whole utterances, certain boundary effects come into operation. The effects tend to 'blur' (to put it crudely for the moment) particularly the consonant sound – and in some cases the consonant sounds – in final and penultimate position in a word. Before we come to transcribing sentences we will consider such effects as assimilation, elision and linkage.

In terms of the transcription exercises included in this chapter, the same provisos apply as mentioned in the introduction to Chapter Eleven and you may want to read through that section again before continuing.

12.2 Symbols used in this chapter

Along with the symbols 'borrowed' from our normal spelling system, there is also a range of symbols, as we saw in Chapter Eight, that have been imported from other alphabets and some which have been purposely invented for use in transcription. These are:

/j/ as in 'yacht' and after:

/k/ as in 'cue' /kjuː/, 'cube' /kjuːb/

/n/ as in 'new' /njuː/, 'neutron' /njuːtrɒn/

/b/ as in 'beautiful' /bjuːtɪfʊl/

/d/ as in 'duty' /djuːtɪ/, 'dupe' /djuːp/

/p/ as in 'pure' /pjʊə/, 'puny' /pjuːnɪ/

/t/ as in 'tube' /tju:b/, 'tuna' /tju:nə/

/v/ as in 'view' /vju:/

/f/ as in 'few' /fju:/, 'fuel' /fjʊəl/

/m/ as in 'mews' /mju:z/, 'muse' /mju:z/

and, as well as these, initially in words like 'union' /ju:nɪən/, 'unique' /ju:ni:k/, 'ewe' /ju:/ and 'you' /ju:/.

Obviously, care has to be taken here to concentrate on how particular words are spoken and, as pointed out in Chapter Eleven, the normal written form is best not referred to, as this often offers little clue as to the presence of /j/.

12.3 Transcription Exercises 9-12

Try this short exercise to practise an awareness of the presence (or absence!) of /j/:

Transcription Exercise 9

e.g. beauty /bju:tɪ/   boon /bu:n/

1. your _____   2. yelp _____   3. music _____

4. moon _____   5. putrid _____   6. pool _____

7. nuisance _____ 8. queue _____   9. coop _____

Going on from this we have:

/θ/ as in thistle

/ð/ as in those

/ʃ/ as in shine

/ʒ/ as in pleasure

/ŋ/ as in thi**ng** and also before velar consonant sounds – i.e. /k/ and /g/ - as in 'wink' /wɪŋk/, 'English' /ɪŋglɪʃ/, 'linguistics' /lɪŋgwɪstɪks/, rather than the ŋ suggested by the spelling.

And finally the affricates:

/tʃ/ as in mu**ch**, ma**tch**

/dʒ/ as in ju**dge** - dʒʌdʒ/. Note here that /dʒ/ often represents the initial sound in words that in conventional spelling start with the letter 'j'.

Transcription Exercise 10

Transcribe those monosyllabic words which incorporate the consonant phonemes that we've just looked at:

e.g. just (adjective) /dʒʌst/

1. jute _____   2. church _____   3. wish _____

4. teeth _____   5. teethe _____   6. treasure _____

7. ceiling _____   8. bank _____   9. charge _____

10. language _____   11. watch _____   12. shrink _____

The Diphthongs

As we stated earlier these sounds involve a glide from one vowel position to another. They are:

Front closing

These start with an initial tongue position mid or back in the mouth and have a forward movement:

/eɪ/ as in <u>A</u>pril /eɪprɪl/

/aɪ/ as in m<u>igh</u>t /maɪt/

/ɔɪ/ as in c<u>oy</u> /kɔɪ/

Back closing

The inverse procedure of the above:

/aʊ/ as in h<u>ow</u> /haʊ/

/əʊ/ as in c<u>o</u>ne /kəʊn/

Centring

These move from either a front or back position to a central one and all terminate with the vowel schwa.

/ɪə/ as in b<u>eer</u> /bɪə/

/ɛə/ as in <u>air</u> /ɛə/

/ʊə/ as in j<u>u</u>ry /dʒʊərɪ/

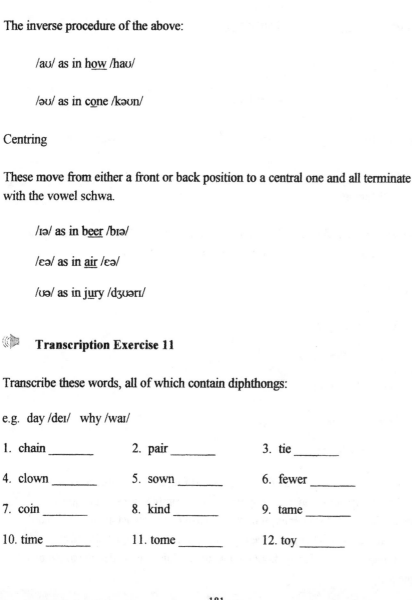 Transcription Exercise 11

Transcribe these words, all of which contain diphthongs:

e.g. day /deɪ/   why /waɪ/

1. chain _____   2. pair _____   3. tie _____

4. clown _____   5. sown _____   6. fewer _____

7. coin _____   8. kind _____   9. tame _____

10. time _____   11. tome _____   12. toy _____

Now have a go at transcribing some di- and polysyllabic words incorporating the consonant and diphthong phonemes we've considered so far:

e.g. juicy /dʒuːsɪ/   general /dʒɛnərəl/

1. oboe _____   2. changing _____   3. failure _____

4. sharing _____ 5. copious _____   6. invidious _____

7. usually _____ 8. Thursday _____   9. station _____

10. chairperson _____ 11. germane _____   12. overcharge _____

The Triphthongs

Vowel sounds that have triphthong realisation have a glide from an initial vowel position to a second and then they centre to end with schwa /ə/.

These are:

/eɪə/ as in pl<u>ayer</u>

/aɪə/ as in f<u>ire</u>

/ɔɪə/ as in l<u>awyer</u>

/aʊə/ as in h<u>our</u>

/əʊə/ as in l<u>ower</u>

Thus we have now covered all the phonemes of English (R.P.) and as stated in the introduction, can now transcribe any word using combinations of the above symbols. So far in this chapter, though, we have been practising on single word transcriptions. This is because when we come to committing whole utterances to paper, things become slightly more complicated. This may be demonstrated by a simple test.

Say the word 'hand'.

Your pronunciation of this will almost certainly be /hænd/.

Now try saying, at normal speed, the sentence:

'Hand me that pencil for a second.'

If you examine your pronunciation of the word 'hand' within this context you will probably find that it differs from its isolated realisation. Most speakers would, in fact, pronounce it as /hæm/. The same thing happens within the 'compound word' **handbag**. In English spoken at normal speed, this would usually be realised as /hæmbæg/.

This little test demonstrates two significant features of ordinary spoken English, **assimilation** and **elision** and it is to these features that we now turn.

12.4 Assimilation

Put simply, assimilation means that certain sounds – most particularly alveolar ones – are susceptible to change depending on what type of sound follows them. They are, as it were, unstable and tend to take on an articulation that in some degree approximates to the phoneme that follows them. Thus we see that in an instance like 'that pair' the /t/ of 'that' is likely to be assimilated by the /p/ in 'pair' and be uttered itself as a /p/ rather than as an alveolar plosive i.e. /ðæp peə/.

The same is true of the /t/ in 'that ball' where again the /t/ is likely to be assimilated to a /p/ - /ðæp bɔːl/.

Assimilation, then, affects the place but, notice, not the manner of articulation. There is no change of voicing condition. Thus in effect what would in isolation be a /t/, in the instances above, 'mutates' to a voiceless bilabial plosive – not a voiced one – even before voiced /b/.

Let's look at /t/ and some other phonemes that are prone to assimilation.

/t/ before bilabials becomes /p/ as in the examples above.

/t/ before velars becomes /k/ as in   'that card' /ðæk kɑːd/
                                            'that guard' /ðæk gɑːd/

/d/ before bilabials becomes /b/ as in 'hard ball' /hɑːb bɔːl/

/d/ before velars becomes /g/ as in 'hard court' /hɑːg kɔːt/

/n/ before bilabials becomes /m/ as in 'pin money' /pɪm mʌnɪ/

/n/ before velars becomes /ŋ/ as in 'thin coat' /θɪŋ kəʊt/

/s/ before sibilants* becomes /ʃ/ as in 'this shoe' /ðɪʃ ʃuː/

/z/ before sibilants* becomes /ʒ/ as in 'those shoes' /ðəʊʒ ʃuːz/

* except /s/ and /z/.

12.5   Elision

If assimilation implies that sounds are affected by their neighbouring phonemes, elision refers to their complete omission. Thus going back to the example of 'handbag' above, we did, in fact, have both assimilation and elision working in tandem. The 'd' here would not normally be pronounced – in other words, it is elided. Since it is elided, this leaves the (potential) /n/ subject to assimilation conditioned by the succeeding /b/, giving /m/ - hence /hæmbæg/.

Elision aids fluency and ease of articulation, operating in contexts where there is likely to be little ambiguity caused by omitting a particular phoneme. Sometimes repeated elision leads to a new phonetic form of a particular word becoming the preferred or standard version. This is true, for example, of words like 'Christmas', 'whistle' and 'castle' where pronouncing the /t/ would, now, be incorrect, despite the fact that historically the /t/ was sounded. This type of elision is known as **historical elision** and only the elided forms are now permissible. However, in rapid everyday speech elision may also occur, as we saw with the 'Hand me that pen ...' example, where the /d/ is elided and the /n/ assimilated. In cases like this we have **contextual elision**. This means that whether or not a particular phoneme is elided is determined by the context and because of this both elided and unelided forms may occur – and, indeed, we do not tend to notice their variable incidence. In very formal speech, elision is less likely to occur than in informal situations. People giving formal-type speeches, for example will speak 'more carefully' (no qualitative judgement implied here) than friends chatting, though this may not always be the case (a rousing political speech is likely to include factors such as elision).

Contextual elision affects primarily /t/, /d/ and /ə/. Examples of this are:

/t/ as in 'fast food' /fɑːs fuːd/

/d/ as in 'bruised pride' /bruːz praɪd/

/ə/ as in 'secretary' /sɛkrətrɪ/ (unelided form /sɛkrətərɪ/)

12.6 Linkage

Linkage, in the sense that we use it here, refers to juncture between words, the former of which ends with potential /r/. What this means is that some words such as 'star', 'sugar', 'for' and so on, which in R.P. and other – but not all – accents of English would normally be pronounced without a /r/ can under certain circumstances 'generate' a /r/ and, via this, be linked to the next word. The main proviso for this happening is that the subsequent word begins with a vowel sound. Thus in a phrase like 'Star of Asia' the words 'star' and 'of' would usually be linked, so instead of the rather halting /stɑː əv eɪʃə/, most speakers would pronounce this /stɑːrəv eɪʃə/. The same is true of the sequence 'for a minute' where the first two words would be spoken as /fərə/. Historically, words that in the written script end with an 'r' (or indeed have an 'r' in them that is not now sounded – 'start', 'farmer' etc) would have had a pronunciation that included it. Hence 'star' would have been pronounced /stɑːr/. Of course, in some accents of English – East Anglian, Scots, American and others – the /r/ phoneme is still part of the citation form of such words. However in accents that are not **rhotic** (rhotic accents are those that have the /r/ today) there is a potential for /r/ to be generated if the boundary between words is vowel sound + 'r' (in the spelling) + vowel sound. Linking /r/, like assimilation and elision aids fluency.

Interestingly enough, when the /r/ began to be dropped from the former standard citation forms of words like 'star', 'lore' etc, new rhymes came into the language.

Whilst 'lore' had not previously been identical in pronunciation to 'law' after this particular language change, it was. This led to another phenomenon – **intrusive /r/**. By analogy to linkage via /r/ in phrases like 'Star of Asia', intrusive /r/ started to be generated in phrases like 'law and order' - /lɔːrə nɔːdə/ (notice, too, how the /d/ in 'and' may well be elided here). Some people consider this particular feature of language to be 'lazy' or 'sloppy' but in linguistic terms it is simply something that constitutes part of everyday spoken English.

/r/ may well be generated within words as well as across word boundaries. Thus we have 'star' /stɑː/ but 'starry' /stɑːrɪ/, 'stir' /stɜː/ but 'stirring' /stɜːrɪŋ/. In cases such as these where the bound morpheme has an initial vowel sound, /r/ will, as a matter of course, be generated.

Let's now look at some transcriptions that include the features that we've just considered.

1.   'That might be a bit problematic.'
     /ðæp maɪp biː ə bɪp prɒbləmætɪk/

2.   'Could we have some salad cream?'
     /kʊb wi hæv sʌm sæləg kriːm/

3.   'He went past the bank and looked for a taxi.'
     /hɪwem paːs ðə bæŋk ən lʊk fərə tæksɪ/

4.   'Shoes should be left by the door.'
     /ʃuːʒ ʃʊb bɪ lɛf baɪ ðə dɔː/

5.   'That cupboard can be used for all important papers.'
     /ðæk kʌbəg kəm bɪ juːzd fərɔːl ɪmpɔːtəm peɪpəz/

🔊 **12.7 Transcription Exercise 13**

In the following utterances, there is potential for elision, assimilation and linkage. Say the utterances to yourself and then have a go at transcribing them, including, where appropriate, these features.

1.   'Can we get coffee here?'

_____

2.   'What possible motive could people have for such things?'

_____

3.   'The police are looking for a red car.'

_____

4.   'For a moment Bob was shocked.'

_____

5.   'I've lost my handbag.'

_____

6.   'It put paid to our plans for a holiday.'

_____

7. 'I don't remember it.'

---

8. 'A cheese and wine party.'

---

9. 'Law and order is an important priority.'

---

10. 'What's your poison?'

12.7 Applications

Again though there is perhaps no one direct application of the principles that we have looked at in this final chapter, there is the important implication that teachers should try to keep their language as authentic as possible when operating in the classroom. Students following programmes of study in English-speaking countries will certainly encounter the features we've considered and need to be prepared for them if communication is not to be impaired. Unnaturally slow speech on the part of the teacher will not highlight phenomena such as assimilation, elision and linkage and, in the long run, will not adequately prime learners for native-speaker interaction. It is not necessarily a high-priority objective to develop an active production of these linguistic features in ESOL learners, though this may occur of its own volition, but a receptive capacity will undoubtedly aid the decoding process.

In conclusion, it is probably worth underlining our initial point that in most situations, teacher-talk is the learner's main vehicle of exposure to spoken English, and therefore it is incumbent upon teachers to provide a model that approximates as much as possible to language use in the situation where learners will actually need it most: outside the classroom.

12.8 Summary

In this chapter we have:

- completed the re-introduction of the remainder of the full set of phonemic symbols for English

- looked at various effects found in connected speech including:

  - linking /r/
  - assimilation
  - elision

- provided some exercises to practise these features in transcription

12.9 Key to the exercises

Transcription exercise 9

1. your …/jɔː/…

2. yelp …/jɛlp/…

3. music …/mjuːzɪk/…

4. moon …/muːn/…

5. putrid …/pjuːtrɪd/…

6. pool …/puːl/…

7. nuisance …/njuːsəns/…

8. queue …/kjuː/…

9. coop …/kuːp/…

Transcription exercise 10

1. jute …/dʒuːt/…

2. church …/tʃɜːtʃ/…

3. wish …/wɪʃ/…

4. teeth …/tiːθ/…

5. teethe …/tiːð/…

6. treasure …/treʒə/…

7. ceiling …/siːlɪŋ/…

8. bank …/bæŋk/…

9. charge /tʃɑːdʒ/…

10. language …/læŋgwɪdʒ/…

11. watch …/wɒtʃ/…

12. shrink …/ʃrɪŋk/…

Transcription exercise 11

1. chain …/tʃeɪn/…

2. pair …/pɛə/…

3. tie …/taɪ/…

4. clown …/klaʊn/…

5. sown …/səʊn/…

6. fewer …/fjʊə/…

7. coin …/kɔɪn/…

8. kind …/kaɪnd/…

9. tame …/teɪm/…

10. time …/taɪm/…

11. tome …/təʊm/…

12. toy …/tɔɪ/…

Transcription exercise 12

1. oboe …/əʊbəʊ/…

2. changing /tʃeɪndʒɪŋ /

3. failure …/feɪljə/…

4. sharing …/ʃɛərɪŋ/…

5. copious …/kəʊpɪəs/…

6. invidious ../ɪnvɪdɪəs/…

7. usually .../juːʒʊəlɪ/...   8. Thursday .../θɜːzdɪ/...   9. station .../steɪʃən/...

10. chairperson /tʒɛəpɜːsən/...   11. germane.../dʒɜːmeɪn/...   12. overcharge
                                                                    .../əʊvətʃɑːdʒ/...

Transcription exercise 13

1. 'Can we get coffee here?'

    .../kəm wɪ gek kɒfɪ hɪə/..

2. 'What possible motive could people have for such things?'

    .../wɒp pɒsɪbəl məʊtɪv kʊb piːpəl hæv fə sʌtʃ θɪŋz/..............................

3. 'The police are looking for a red car.'

    .../ðə pəliːs ə lʊkɪŋ fərə reg kɑː/..

4. 'For a moment Bob was shocked.'

    .../fərə məʊməm bɒb wəʒ ʃɒkt/..

5. 'I've lost my handbag.'

    .../aɪv lɒs maɪ hæmbæg/..

6. 'It put paid to our plans for a holiday.'

    .../ɪp pʊp peɪd tʊ aʊə plænz fərə hɒlɪdeɪ/...

192

7. 'I don't remember it.'

   .../aɪ dəʊn rɪmembərɪt/...

8. 'A cheese and wine party.'

   .../ə tʃiːz əm waɪm paːtɪ/..

9. 'Law and order is an important priority.'

   .../lɔːrənɔːdərɪzən ɪmpɔːtəm praɪɒrɪtɪ/..

10. 'What's your poison?'

   .../wɒtʃ jɔː pɔɪzən/..

Postscript 1

International English and objectives for the teaching of pronunciation

The purpose of this chapter is to examine the implications for phonological objectives in a language programme within the context of increasing internationalisation of English. As English becomes in effect the default language of the world and more and more people begin to learn and acquire it, it will clearly become increasingly common for communication in English to take place between non-native speakers. For example it is no longer rare for a Japanese business person to conduct commercial interactions with a German, French or Brazilian business person through the medium of the English language. Teachers of English must bear this in mind. In Chapter One we touched upon intelligibility and the question of what accent learners should aim for. We mentioned the idea of clarity being key. It is important for us as teachers to provide learners with exposure to different models of accent, or perhaps types, so that they achieve clarity of both understanding and production in a variety of settings.

If the teacher is teaching a mixed language group, as often they are, in English speaking countries, then the provision of a mixture of accents is not going to be a problem. If on the other hand, the teacher is teaching a single language group as would usually be the case in a non-English speaking country, then provision of different types of accent becomes more problematic. All learners tend to develop a tolerance for their teachers' accents. This is one of the reasons that teachers are encouraged to utilise audio and video cassettes to give learners exposure to the accents of other native English speakers. This is beneficial to a degree of course, but does not solve the problem alluded to above. Unless learners have the opportunity to hear a range of non-native accents it will be difficult for them to easily cope with and comprehend these accents when they encounter them.

For monolingual groups one way forward is for teachers to ensure that they play tapes and dialogues which feature non-native accents. There are a few published materials that do have a mix of native and non-native accents, but often it may be necessary for the teacher to devise their own by recording speakers on the television or radio.

To a certain extent this begs the question of what a 'final' accent objective should be. Again, as we mentioned in Chapter One, we should be careful to be neutral in what we expect learners to do in this area. In the end, though, we must also face up to the fact that learners expect us as teachers to deliver the goods. They need to feel confident with different sorts of speaker, both native and non-native. It is no longer the case that Received Pronunciation is perceived as being the only accent of English that learners should be aiming for. This of course applies to British English but the same kind of idea of native-like pronunciation is true of all types of English, American, Australian and so on.

This move to a more pragmatic, indeed one might even characterise it as liberal, approach to the teaching of pronunciation seems to have been a natural ingredient of the communicative approach to language teaching and the rise in the 'desirability' of a non-native speaker's non-native accent mirrors the rise in the number of communicative classrooms around the world. So on the one hand then, this liberalisation can be seen as a positive thing. On the other hand, however, it does give us as teachers something of a dilemma when it comes to knowing what to aim for instead. Terms such as communicative effectiveness and comfortable intelligibility are often banded about, but what in the end do they mean? The different sorts of classroom mentioned above necessarily mean that comfortable intelligibility is a relative concept. Monolingual classes and multilingual classes produce different forms of comfortable intelligibility. The degree of comfort of intelligibility that experienced teachers of ESOL display and can afford their learners, is not the same as that which would be experienced by the ordinary English speaker in the street as we have mentioned before. Similarly, a learner who has only ever heard their teacher's accent or narrow range of accents at least, may find it difficult to tune into 'new' accents.

Clearly there are more questions than answers here, but their resolution should prove interesting as time passes and the speakership of English increases.

Postscript 2

The following are a few examples of the type of question that candidates for the Trinity College London LTCL Diploma might be asked during the oral interview part of the examination. Space is provided for you to make notes and then some illustrative answers follow.

LTCL Interviews

General Questions

1. What do you understand by complementary distribution? Illustrate your answer with examples from English.

2. What is the difference between phonetics and phonology? Which of the two is more centrally the concern of language teachers and why?

3. How does voicing act as a distinctive feature in English? - give plenty of examples.

4. What is a phoneme? - how many are there in English? - which is the most common phoneme?

5. What is the difference between segmental and suprasegmental phonology? Which of these two areas seems more important for English language teachers?

6. What is R.P.? Does the existence of this accent have any implications for English language teaching?

7. What is the difference between an accent and a dialect?

8. What is an allophone - give some examples of allophones in English.

9. What purposes are served in your view by introducing students to the phonemic symbols that you know?

10. What do you understand by the term free variation in the context of the phonological description of a language. Give an example from English.

Postscript 3

Answers to General Questions

1. Complementary distribution refers to the way in which allophones occur in phonetically predictable contexts. For example the /t/ in 'twin' is labialised because it is immediately followed by labio-velar /w/. The lips are rounded throughout the production of the /t/ allophone in anticipation of the subsequent sound. The /t/ allophone in 'tip', on the other hand, does not have this lip-rounding and is produced purely with contact on the alveolar ridge. In fact, for this allophone, the lips are relatively spread because of the following vowel, /I/. Thus we can say that the two allophones are in complementary distribution to one another. Neither would occur in the others 'natural home'. There are some minor exceptions to this rule when free variation may occur, but generally speaking, each allophone member of any one given phoneme set will complement rather than contradict or contrast with any other allophone from that particular family of sounds.

2. Phonetics is the systematic study of individual speech sounds and their inherent qualities. It focuses on the fine detail of articulation. For example, the difference between alveolar (t) in English and dental (t) in French is a comparative phonetic qualitative distinction. Phonology, whilst encapsulating this aspect of pronunciation, is a broader area of study and includes things such as suprasegmental features, stress, rhythm and intonation. Phonology is therefore more widely focused than phonetics and it is possible to argue that it is of more central use and value to the language teacher. Subtle inaccuracies at the level of the individual sound can be relatively easily tolerated by various domain speakers, whilst inaccuracies in the area of stress and intonation can be much harder to accommodate by those very same speakers.

Phonology is also taken to mean the systematic study of the speech patterns and sound-types of a particular language. It is, then, possible to talk, for instance, of the phonology of Russian.

3. Voicing acts as a means of doubling up the inventory of certain types of articulation. The fact that voice can be added to a type of articulation means that, for example, /t/ and /d/ can be perceived as separate sounds in English. The /t/ sound has no voicing because the vocal cords do not vibrate during its production. The /d/ sound, on the other hand, does have voice because air is forced through the vocal cords during its articulation, forcing them to vibrate. Voice adds depth and 'bassiness' to a sound relative to its voiceless partner articulation. Similarly in English we can distinguish /p/, /k/ and /g/ and many other pairs of sounds, through the fact that one partner is voiceless and the other is voiced. It should be pointed out that this phenomenon is specific to certain types of consonant sound and does not apply to vowel sounds, all of which are voiced.

4. A phoneme is an idealised sound type that encompasses the various allophones that are actually phonetically realised under conditioned circumstances when language is spoken. There are 44 in English – 49 if triphthongs are counted – and these sounds make up the inventory of articulations that the native speaker would recognise as distinct and potentially the building bricks of words. It is, therefore, possible to argue that phonemes have a kind of psychologically reality for native speakers (whereas allophones usually don't). A phoneme is the smallest segment of speech which, when adjusted one for another, has the potential to make a meaningful difference between words. For example, 'pin' and 'bin' (phonemically transcribed as 'pɪn/ and bɪn/ are perceived by speakers of the English language to be distinct and related to quite different concepts. Phonemes can form what are known as minimal pairs. These are items like the one just instanced, where two words are distinguished by a single unit of meaningful sound (meaningful here doesn't refer to semantic value but to semantico-phonetic significance). 'Pin' and 'bin' just like, say, 'hay' and 'say' differ as words from one another by just one sound. These are said to be minimal pairs and the fact that this can happen in a language is one of the more central tests of what does or does not constitute a phoneme in that language. It should be remembered that phonemes are language specific and that different languages can divide the putative articulatory range of sounds in quite different ways. An example of this would be Japanese where /l/ and /r/ are allophones, whilst in English they are distinct phonemes. This helps to explain why Japanese learners of English tend to have problems when attempting to discriminate between /l/ and /r/ both receptively and productively.

What needs to be borne in mind, is that phonemes are not real sounds but a generic label applied to a group of language specific sound types that concur in quality to a large degree and are perceived or proficient speakers to be 'as one'. The most common phoneme in the English language is schwa /ə/.

5. Segmental phonology is concerned with investigating the properties of individual sound types that occur in the world's languages. It is focused at the level of the segment – in other words the phoneme and its related allophones. Segmental phonology is concerned with the articulatory and acoustic qualities of single items of the speech stream. This concern may be language specific or it may involve language comparison, as with, for example, contrastive phonetic analysis of English and German to discover patterns of similarity of common phonetic root (schwimmen = to swim, schwingen = to swing etc).

6. Received pronunciation exists as a regionless accent of English. In this regard it is relatively unusual. It is associated with BBC English and the media in general as well as public schools in the UK. It is very common as a citation form for pronunciation in dictionaries both for native speakers and for learners of the language. It is also common in TESOL materials such as tapes, videos and coursebooks. Teachers should, perhaps, acknowledge it as a kind of neutral accent – though some qualification of this might be needed in sociolinguistic terms. Teachers need not, of course, be RP speakers and shouldn't feel the need to adopt RP if they are not users of this accent.

7. An accent is defined by phonological distinctiveness only. In other words, accent is only the sounds uttered by a speaker of the language and those features that delineate their local or national constituency. An accent can, therefore, be described as being indicative of a particular speech community or indicative of a particular set of learners of a language – speaking English with an Italian accent for example. A localised single speech community example would be the lack of use of the phoneme /ʌ/ in most northern accents of Britain compared to those of the South East. Where such speakers would pronounce 'cup' as /kʌp/, many speakers from the North would rent this as /kʊp/.

Dialect, on the other hand, includes pronunciation but also encompasses lexical, syntactical, grammatical and semantic differences. This means that dialects tend to be more opaque than accents: more difficult for 'outsiders' to understand and interpret. This is because dialects might, for instance, actually have different words to refer to the same thing but these words are shared by a specific set of domain speakers and can be entirely unknown to those from beyond the region where the dialect is used. In Britain, dialects are nowhere near as common as they used to be due to increased social and geographical mobility and mass education and the influence of the broadcast media. There are still traits of dialect that survive through, particularly at a lexical level. For example, in Sheffield a 'breadcake' is the equivalent of a 'bap' or, in American English, a 'bun'. Similarly 'nesh' is an adjective that is used pejoratively to indicate someone who cannot easily tolerate cold weather conditions. Another example is the term used by the former Prime Minister, Margaret Thatcher, who once famously described the then leader of the Opposition, Neil Kinnock, of being 'frit' – a dialectal word used in the area and around Grantham in South Lincolnshire for 'frightened' – over a political issue. Grammatical differences, though rarer, do also still exist – the continued use of the generally archaic 'thee', 'thou' and 'thine' in some accents in Yorkshire in the UK for example. Dialects can exist even at a national level between speakers of the same language: the fact that Austrian speakers will greet each other with the phrase 'Grüss Got', whilst German speakers use (amongst other forms) 'Guten Tag', being a case in point.

8. An allophone is a conditioned speech sound that occurs in predictable phonetic environments. For example, the two different articulations of the idealised phoneme /l/ in the word 'little' are allophones. The first sound, at the beginning of a word and preceding a vowel is known as 'light' (l), whilst the final sound occurring at the end of a word and before a pause is termed 'dark' (l). The difference between the two is that the first (l) has the tongue relatively flat in the mouth, whereas the second has the body of the tongue raised up towards the soft palate. In other words, dark (l) is velarised and light (l) is not. These sounds, though, occur in complementary distribution to one another and do not have the potential to contrast or change the perception of a word. In Australian English, for example, light (l) doesn't occur but the fact that both (l)s are rendered dark by Australian speakers doesn't lead to any lack of comprehension on the part of proficient speakers of the language – they may subconsciously or consciously register that there is a difference between this pronunciation and their own but they are unaware of what the technicalities of this difference are. Allophones, therefore, do not have the potential to change

meaning, but are unconsciously used in natural phonetic environments by native speakers. Any one phoneme of a language can have very many allophones depending on its incidence of occurrence.

9. The question of whether to introduce students to phonemic script is really one of when and to what degree. If learners are unfamiliar with Roman script and are struggling to master it at the beginner level, it could be argued that presenting them with the extra burden of having to learn phonemic script would not only be confusing but, quite possibly, counter-productive. The argument, then, would hold that the teaching of phonemic script should only be undertaken once the ordinary writing and spelling system has become a familiar property. This is not to say though, that some symbols might not be usually taught. This again will depend on the type of learner that one teaches. It may be advantageous to teach a small subset of the overall transcription system, because being able to refer to certain sounds via symbols could be of direct help. Speakers of those languages which don't, for example, have either /θ/ or /ð/ as English does, and who consequently have problems with these sounds might be helped to a small, but nevertheless useful extent, by being taught the symbols for them, so that the teacher can refer directly to them through, say, board work. There is also a strong case for teaching learners the symbol for schwa /ə/ as this is the most common sound in the English language and is represented by many different spelling combinations.

For more proficient learners it is certainly possible to put a good case for teaching them, or encouraging them to learn the whole of the phonetic transcription system, as this provides them with a ready means of working out the pronunciation of a new word that they check up on in good learners' dictionaries in the absence of the teacher. It is also handy for noting down in class the pronunciation of oddly spelt words. Having an awareness of the transcription system can, in the long run, only serve to increase learners' appreciation of the whole of the pronunciation system of the English language, particularly perhaps in the areas of stress and consequently help ultimately with rhythm and intonation.

10. Free variation refers to the phenomenon whereby in certain contexts allophones and, sometimes words, can be substituted one for another. An example of those at an allophonic level would be the repeated uttering of the word 'pot' which

would lead to slight variations in the rendering of the last sound in the word. Sometimes the /t/ would have plosion, sometimes not. Sometimes there might be incomplete plosion and sometimes an ejective (t) would occur. Whilst allophones do not normally occur in the same phonetic environment (because they usually exist in complementary distribution to one another) in these special circumstances they may do. At the level of the word there may also be free variation as when two or more acceptable pronunciations exist. An example of this would be 'controversy' where some speakers stress the first syllable and others the second, and indeed some speakers use both forms randomly. The same could be said of the word 'grass' sometimes pronounced as /grɑːs/ and sometimes as /græs/. The first allophonic version of this phenomenon has little or no significance to teachers or learners of English, but the second could be important in that learners may need to appreciate different accents or pronunciations and the fact that these can vary slightly and still refer to the same thing.

Glossary of Technical and Semi-Technical Terms

Accent

A particular systematic variation of the phonological system of a language. Typically, accents tend to be geographically located, e.g. a South Yorkshire accent or a Birmingham accent, but occasionally (and this is especially the case in English), a non-geographical accent can occur such as R.P. It is important to recognise that an accent is entirely a matter of pronunciation. Other variations within a language such as systematic differences of grammar or vocabulary go together with accent to make up a dialect. Technically, the word 'accent' is never used (as it sometimes is in general usage) to mean stress.

Affricate

A kind of consonant sound which is a combination of a stop and a fricative – in that order – and in which these two components have the same place of articulation. There are only two of these in English - /tʃ/ and /dʒ/.

Allophone

One way to understand the concept of the allophone is to consider it as a member of a 'phoneme family'. In other words it is a sound that, when focused on, can be demonstrated to be different from other very similar sounds but doesn't ever replace them to produce different words. An example would be the first consonant sound in the words 'kill' and 'call'. We would transcribe these words in a phonemic transcription as /kɪl/ and /kɔːl/. In other words we consider those two first consonant sounds as being the same. If we articulate them slowly and carefully, however, we can demonstrate that they are substantially different – particularly in articulatory terms. The difference, however, is not significant in a communicative sense. If we produced the wrong /k/ sound at the beginning of those words (easier said than done!) we would simply sound strange – we would not produce a different word.

Articulator

Part of the anatomy, which, whatever its primary biological purpose(s), is used to create speech sounds, e.g. the tongue, the velum, the lips etc.

Assimilation

An effect on consonant sounds (almost always in word-final position) where the **place of articulation** of a following consonant sound transfers to it, e.g. bad boy ... /bæb bɔɪ/.

Auxiliaries

A class of verb including primary auxiliaries such as 'be, have, do' and modal auxiliaries such as 'must, can' etc. These are of particular interest to phonologists in English because of their tendency to take up unstressed positions in sentences.

Broad

An adjective used to describe transcriptions of speech which only account for **phonemic** features and thus ignore any acoustic or articulatory variations which are not significant with regard to the transmission of meaning.

Cardinal vowels

The largely imaginary series of vowel sounds set by phoneticians as reference points against which real vowel sounds can be measured and described.

Complementary distribution

The occurrence in a language of a particular set of speech sounds in such a way that they never contrast with each other in terms of changing meaning. For example there are evidently at least two different /l/ sounds in English – the so called clear 'l' (e.g. /lɪp/) and the so called dark 'l' (e.g. /pɪl/). In English, however, the latter never occurs in word-initial position and the former never occurs in word-final position except when followed immediately by a vowel-initial word, when the 'normal' word boundary may be suppressed. These two allophones of /l/ are, therefore, said to be in complementary distribution.

Consonant

A speech sound in which part of its quality is due to the interference of the air stream by one or more articulators. The interference may take the form of complete or partial temporary closure.

Consonant cluster

A series of adjacent consonant sounds either within a word e.g. /sp/ in the words 'space', 'lisping' and 'cusp' or resulting from the boundaries between words in connected speech – e.g. /sp/ in 'this pen'. Phonologists interest themselves in this matter (often referred to as phonotactics) since the occurrence and distribution of particular consonant clusters tends to be quite different from one language to another and can, therefore, represent a considerable learning burden.

Content words

Those words in a language like English which, in contrast to structure words, carry the main information content of utterances. These are of interest to phonologists since they are generally stressed and thus have a predictable effect on the rhythm of an utterance.

Contrastive stress

The employment of special stress in an utterance in order to indicate either that two elements in the utterance are being contrasted or that one element in the utterance is being contrasted with another element elsewhere in the discourse or understood from the context e.g.

A: Would you care for tea or coffee?
B: I'd love some <u>tea</u>.

Diachronic

This is an adjective used to describe studies, particularly of language, which attempt to view the object of study over a period of time. Thus, a diachronic view of English would be taking into account the historical development of the language, the languages out of which it has developed and the continuing process of language change.

Diphthong

A single vowel phoneme in which the tongue (and possibly other articulators) moves during the execution of the sound so that the resulting sound is a smooth transition from one vowel sound to another.

Disyllabic

An adjective used to describe words which are made up of two syllables.

EFL

English as a Foreign Language (TEFL = The Teaching of EFL).

Elision

This phenomenon is the actual loss of a speech sound (usually a consonant sound). This can occur either within a word and probably for historical reasons (historical elision) – e.g. the/t/ in 'fasten' or at a word boundary (contextual elision) – e.g. 'the last day' /ðə lɑːs deɪ/.

ESOL

This is an acronym which, whatever its original purpose, seems to be replacing EFL. It stands for English to Speakers of Other Languages. (TESOL = The Teaching of ESOL).

Fortis

The fortis consonant sounds are those which require a relatively high amount of muscular effort in their production. (There are other definitions but these tend towards phonetic rather than phonemic values, so we will skip them.) The opposite is lenis. In English the fortis consonant sounds are all voiceless.

Fricative

When two articulatory organs get close enough to create friction in the air stream passing between them but not close enough to stop it, the result is a fricative consonant sound. Examples from English are:

/f/, /v/, /θ/, /ð/, /s/, /z/, /ʃ/, /ʒ/, /x/ (as in Scottish 'lo**ch**')

Frictionless continuants

/r/ is a frictionless continuant. Although it lacks many of the obvious characteristics of a consonant sound, it has the functional status of a consonant sound. Other frictionless continuants in English are /w/ and /j/. /w/ and /j/ are also often labelled semi-vowels.

Function words

Those words which unlike content words do not add much to utterances by way of meaning but provide syntactic information. Function words include most of the closed word classes such as auxiliary verbs, determiners, pronouns, prepositions and conjunctions.

Head

This term is used in the analysis of intonation to identify part of an utterance. It applies to that part of an utterance which stretches from the first stressed syllable to the nucleus – e.g.

> We've been <u>travelling through</u> France this year.

Intonation

The element of phonology concerned with the use of pitch – in other words the system which determines the various musical notes at which different parts of utterances are said.

Lenis

The opposite of fortis, this adjective is used to describe consonant sounds in which there is relatively little breath force (see also 'fortis') – such consonant sounds include in English all the voiced consonant sounds.

Linkage

Words ending in their written form with 'r' do not normally correspond with a pronounced /r/ in that position in R.P. Linkage, however, is the process of re-establishing this /r/ in connected speech when the following sound is a vowel sound.

For example notice the difference in realisation of the two 'r's in:

Father and mother   /fɑːðərənmʌðə/

Minimal pair

A pair of utterances (usually single words) which have a single phonological element (usually a phoneme) that is different – thus:

raid /reɪd/   laid /leɪd/

Longer utterances may be devised to extend the context – e.g.:

Sport is absolutely essential.
Support is absolutely essential.

or to illustrate suprasegmental features – e.g.:

Open the window. (request)
Open the window. (command)

(where the lines indicate the intonation pattern)

Minimal pairs are used by language teachers to help their learners focus on discrete features of the phonology of the target language and to generate practice in the discrimination and the accurate production of those features.

Modal auxiliaries

A set of auxiliary verbs in English including 'must', 'can' etc which have a range of meanings some of which are considered to reflect the intention of the speaker. The value of modal auxiliaries is often reflected in the amount of stress they attract in speech, for example,

> I can do it. /aɪ kən duː ɪt/
> I can do it. /aɪ kæn duː ɪt/
> She can be very difficult at times.
> /ʃɪ kəm bɪ verɪ dɪfɪkəlt ət taɪmz/

Monophthong

A class of vowel sound in which there is a single position of the tongue, lips and lower jaw during its production. Most vowel sounds in English are monophthongs (as opposed to diphthongs and triphthongs) and some languages have only monophthongs in their vowel systems.

Monosyllabic

An adjective used to describe words which are composed of a single syllable, e.g. 'go', 'knight'.

Narrow

An adjective used to describe transcriptions of speech in which more phonetic detail is included than is strictly necessary if only the information relevant to the communicative act being performed were being represented. For example, the feature of aspiration, though unnecessary in a phonemic transcription of English, (since no two words are distinguished by the presence or absence of this feature alone) would routinely be indicated in a narrow or phonetic transcription.

Nasal

This adjective is used to describe both the air stream and the speech sounds produced when the air stream is diverted through the nasal passages rather than or as well as through the oral cavity as a result of the lowering of the velum.

Non-rhotic

The many accents of English can be divided into two major groups – rhotic and non-rhotic. The latter are those in which /r/ does not normally occur in word-final positions or before other consonant sounds: e.g.:

Parker = /pɑːkə/ not /pɑːrkər/ in a non-rhotic accent.

Nucleus

The label for the most prominent syllable in an intonation group and thus the syllable at which the most significant pitch variation in the intonation group occurs or begins, e.g.:

We've been travelling through <u>France</u> this year.

It is also used to refer to the central phoneme in a syllable.

Onomatopoeia

The unusual phenomenon of a word in a language actually mimicking the sound of the thing that it represents. Decisions about whether a word really is onomatopoeic or not are often rather subjective and frequently not upheld by diachronic evidence but examples of words in English claimed to be onomatopoeic include 'to creak', 'a **clap** of thunder', 'cuckoo' etc.

Periphrasis

The term used to label the device available in most languages to manipulate word order in order to change the function or the meaning of an utterance.

Phatic communion

Not every utterance used communicatively is destined to elicit or convey information. Language is frequently used for other social purposes. Language used for purposes such as acknowledging the presence of others (e.g. 'Wotcher!' or 'Good afternoon, ladies and gentlemen'), exchanging greetings or reinforcing social solidarity etc is covered by the term phatic communion).

Phoneme

A phoneme is the smallest unit of sound in the speech system of any language which can, if exchanged for another phoneme, convert one word into another.

Phonemic

A level of analysis of the phonology of a language which stops at the point where variations in sound cease to have any significant communicative effect.

Phonetic

A level of analysis of the sound systems of languages which aims to account for **all** variations in sound whether or not they are communicatively significant in any particular language.

Phonology

This word has two related meanings. Originally it meant the **study** of the sound system of a particular language and it continues to retain this meaning. It has, however, gained an additional meaning by extension and is now frequently used to mean that sound system itself e.g. the phonology of English, the phonology of Swahili etc.

Plosive

Plosives are a class of consonant sound in which the air stream is actually stopped for a short time and then 'explosively' released. Examples of plosives in English are: /p/, /b/, /t/ and /d/.

Polar questions

These are often, also, referred to as 'yes/no questions' and are, predictably those questions which can be answered by 'yes' or 'no'. There are a variety of ways in which these can be formed – e.g. by inversion of subject and verb –

> Are you mad?

or without such inversion but with a characteristic intonation –

> This is the bedroom?

or by adding a question tag –

> You're from Belgium, aren't you?

In all cases, however, they attract the attention of the phonologist and the teacher/learner of English because of their characteristic rising intonation tune.

Polysyllabic

An adjective to describe words which have more than one syllable (often, however, because of the availability of the term disyllabic, this adjective is taken to mean having more than two syllables).

Pre-head

This term is used in the analysis of intonation to identify part of an utterance. It applies to that part of an utterance which precedes the first stressed syllable – e.g.

<u>We've been</u> travelling through France this year.

Prominence

The umbrella term used to describe the collection of phonological features which combine to make a particular syllable, word or other stretch of an utterance more salient than its surroundings. These phonological features include:

    pitch change
    volume
    muscular effort etc.

Received pronunciation

A non-regional accent of English which has traditionally resulted from the educational process in certain settings. Although R.P. itself has a number of variations it is generally associated with a particular class and certain occupations rather than with the inhabitants of any special geographical area.

Rhotic

The many accents of English can be divided into two major groups – rhotic and non-rhotic. The former are those in which the consonant sound /r/ can occur in word-final positions or before other consonant sounds, e.g.:

Parker = /pɑːrkər/ not /pɑːkə/ in a rhotic accent.

Rhythm

The fairly regular occurrence of stressed syllables in utterances in a so-called stress-timed language like English implies the relative compression of the surrounding unstressed syllables. This combination of features is often referred to as rhythm though it would be wrong to expect normal utterances to be 'rhythmic' in the musical sense of the word other than by the accidental arrangement of equal numbers of stressed and unstressed syllables in a particular sequence.

Schwa

This word has been borrowed from Hebrew (or perhaps Ivrit) by phoneticians and in common with other words transliterated from other scripts, it enjoys a variety of spellings in English. You may well see it spelt Shwa or Schwah or Shwah. It is the name given the vowel phoneme /ə/. The sound has two distinctions in the phonology of English. Firstly it is the most common of the vowel phonemes and secondly it is the only phoneme to have acquired a name.

Segmental

An adjective used to describe phonological description and analysis at the level of the phoneme. It contrasts with supra-segmental which is used to describe stretches of speech sounds of longer duration. The actual dividing line between the two areas is a little grey and studies of consonant clusters, for example, tend to be included under the segmental rather than the supra-segmental heading.

Stop

This is the complete temporary closure of the air stream and is an important component of many consonant sounds.

Stress

This is the relative force with which particular sounds are articulated. Acoustically it is normally identified in terms of relative volume. In this book we have identified two levels of stressing – stressed (strong) and unstressed (weak).

Stress-timed

Some languages, English more than most, manipulate the potential of their stress systems. This may mean giving words different meanings depending on whether they are stressed or not, or even allowing the number of stressed syllables in an utterance to largely determine how long that utterance will take to be said. This latter exploitation of the stress system leads to certain languages being described as stress-timed.

Supra-segmental

An adjective used to describe the analysis of stretches of speech sounds larger than phonemes. It is thus an umbrella adjective frequently used to describe studies of such features as stress, intonation and rhythm.

Syllabic

An adjective used to describe certain consonant sounds in certain positions which have certain vowel-like qualities enabling them to constitute a full syllable. In English syllabic consonants occur most commonly in word-final position and are marked in transcription with a short vertical line just below the consonant concerned, e.g.:

/kɪtn̩/ (kitten)

/lɪtl̩/ (little)

Syllable

A syllable is a vowel sound (possibly in isolation – e.g. 'I' but more commonly with a preceding and/or following consonant sound or consonant cluster.) Physiologically, syllables coincide with pulses of air from the lungs. Very rarely English provides us with examples of vowel-free syllables like 'pssssst!'.

Synchronic

A cross-sectional view of a language as opposed to a longitudinal one. In other words a view of a language which does not take into account its historical development but instead tries to account for it as a set of systems existing at a particular point in time (most commonly the present).

Tail

This term is used in the analysis of intonation to identify part of an utterance. It applies to that part of an utterance which follows the nucleus, e.g.:

We've been travelling through France <u>this year</u>.

TEFL

See EFL.

TESOL

See ESOL.

Triphthong

A single vowel phoneme in which the tongue (and possibly other articulators) move twice during the execution of the sound so that the resulting sound is a smooth transition from one vowel sound to another and then to a third.

Voice

Vibration during the production of speech sounds of the vocal cords. This is an important feature of the phonology of English and its absence or presence, for example, is one of the things that accounts for the distinction between /p/ (unvoiced) and /b/ (voiced) together with various other pairs of consonant sounds. Voice is always a feature of vowel sounds in normal speech.

Vowel

In this book we have tried to use this word consistently to mean one of the five letters of the alphabet (a, e, i, o and u) which are used to represent vowel sounds in writing in English.

Vowel sound

A phoneme produced without closure of a friction within the airstream.

Wh-questions

These are questions which in English begin with a 'wh-word' such as 'What, Why, Where' etc. It is important to note that the question word 'How' together with compound forms beginning with how (e.g. How much, How far etc) are included in this category despite their spelling. These question forms are of interest to phonologists because of their characteristic falling intonation tune. Most languages mark most questions with a rising tune and so teachers of English often have to devote some time to the acquisition of falling tunes for these questions by their learners.

Appendix A

The transcription symbols used in this book

Consonant sounds:

/ b / as in bed

/ f / as in fish

/ h / as in hope

/ l / as in love

/ n / as in near

/ s / as in sun

/ v / as in view

/ r / as in run

/ j / as in you

/ ð / as in then

/ ʒ / as in measure, and beige

/ tʃ / as in chin and pitch

/ d / as in door

/ g / as in girl

/ k / as in cat and kite

/ m / as in money

/ p / as in pen

/ t / as in tie

/ z / as in zoo

/ w / as in win

/ θ / as in thin

/ ʃ / as in shoe

/ ŋ / as in wing

/ dʒ / as in gin and just

Vowel sounds

monophthongs

/ i: / as in t<u>ea</u> and s<u>ee</u>m

/ ɪ / as in t<u>i</u>n and p<u>i</u>t

/ ɛ / as in p<u>e</u>t

/ æ / as in c<u>a</u>t

/ ɑ: / as in c<u>ar</u>t

/ ɒ / as in p<u>o</u>t

/ ɔ: / as in p<u>our</u>

/ ʊ / as in g<u>oo</u>d and p<u>u</u>t

/ u: / as in f<u>oo</u>d and tr<u>ue</u>

/ ʌ / as in c<u>u</u>p and p<u>u</u>n

/ ə / as in <u>a</u>like and moth<u>er</u>

/ ɜ: / as in b<u>ir</u>d and sl<u>ur</u>

diphthongs

/ eɪ / as in p<u>ay</u>

/ aɪ / as in h<u>igh</u>

/ ɔɪ / as in b<u>oy</u>

/ aʊ / as in n<u>ow</u>

/ əʊ / as in s<u>o</u> and <u>o</u>pen

/ ɪə / as in d<u>ear</u>

/ ɛə / as in c<u>are</u>

/ ʊə / as in c<u>ure</u>

triphthongs

/ eɪə / as in pl<u>ayer</u>

/ aɪə / as in h<u>ire</u>

/ ɔɪə / as in s<u>oya</u>

/ aʊə / as in c<u>ower</u>

/əʊə/ as in s<u>ower</u>

Bibliography

Abercrombie, D.,	*Elements of General Phonetics.* Edinburgh University Press (1967)
Baker, Ann,	*Ship or Sheep.* Cambridge University Press (1981)
	Tree or Three. Cambridge University Press (1982)
	Introducing English Pronunciation. Cambridge University Press (1982)
Bald, W-D., Cobb, D., and Schwarz, A.,	*Active Grammar.* Longman (1986)
Bolinger, Dwight,	*Intonation and its Parts.* Edward Arnold (1985)
Brazil, David, Coulthard, Malcolm, and Johns, Catherine,	*Discourse Intonation and Language Teaching.* Longman (1980)
Brown, Adam (ed),	*Teaching English Pronunciation.* Routledge (1991)
Chomsky, N., and Halle, M.,	*The Sound Pattern of English.* Harper and Row (1968)
	Collins COBUILD Essential English Dictionary. Collins (1988)
Cruttenden, Alan,	*Intonation.* Cambridge University Press (1986)
Crystal, David,	*Prosodic Systems and Intonation in English.* Cambridge University Press (1969)
Dickerson, Wayne B.,	*Orthography as a Pronunciation Resource,* World Englishes Vol. 6, No. 1 pp 11-20 (1987)
Gimson, A. C.,	*Everyman's English Pronouncing Dictionary.* London: Dent (1967)
Gimson, A. C., Edward Arnold	*An Introduction to the Pronunciation of English.* (1980)
Graham, Carolyn,	*Jazz Chants.* Oxford University Press (1978)

Graham, Carolyn,   *Grammarchants: more jazz-chants.* Oxford University Press (1993)

Greenbaum, Sidney, and Quirk, Randolph,   *A Student's Grammar of the English Language.* Longman (1990)

Haycraft, B.,   *The Teaching of Pronunciation.* Longman (1971)

Hubicka, O.,   'Why bother about phonology?' **in** *Practical English Teaching,* 1/1. (1980)

Jones, Daniel,   *The Pronunciation of English.* Cambridge University Press (1966)

Kenworthy, Joanne,   *Teaching English Pronunciation.* Longman (1987)

Ladefoged, Peter,   *A Course in Phonetics.* Harcourt Brace Jovanovich (1982)

Larsen-Freeman, Diane,   *Techniques and Principles in Language Teaching.* Oxford   University Press (1986)

Leech, Geoffrey, Svartvik, Jan,   *A Communicative Grammar of English.* Longman and (1975)

Lindstromberg, Seth   *The Recipe Book: practical ideas for the language classroom.* (ed), Longman (1990)

MacCarthy, Peter,   *The Teaching of Pronunciation.* Cambridge University Press (1978)

Mittyman, Larry,   *Phonology. Theory and Analysis.* Holt Reinhart Winston (1975)

Monfries, Helen,   *Oral Drills in Sentence Patterns.* Macmillan (1963)

O'Connor, J. D.,   *Better English Pronunciation.* Cambridge University Press (1980)

     Phonetics. Penguin (1973)

O'Connor, J. D., and Arnold, G. F.,   *Intonation of Colloquial English.* 2nd Edition. Longman (1973)

Pennington, Martha C.   *Phonology in English language teaching: an international approach.* Longman (1996)

Roach, Peter,   *English Phonetics and Phonology.* Cambridge University Press   (1983)

Rogerson, Pamela, and Gilbert, Judy B.,   *Speaking Clearly* (Student's Book and Teacher's Book). Cambridge University Press (1990)

Swan, Michael, and Smith, Bernard,   *Learner English.* Cambridge University Press (1987)

Thompson, Ian,   *Intonation Practice.* Oxford University Press (1981)

Trask, R.L.   *A Dictionary of Phonetics and Phonology.* Routledge (1996)

Wells, J. C., and Colson, Greta,   *Practical Phonetics.* Pitman (1971)